EXTRAORDINARY WELLNESS
PRESENTS

CODE GRAPE *Culture*

A Sister-Invoked, Biblical, Support
Intervention for This Crisis We Call Life!

Tonya Lincoln

Aimee Rhodes, Natalyia Rutherford, Ann Sullivan,
Emily Bryant, Kate Jordan, Amy Isom, & Shari Walker

Edited by AMZ KDP Book.

Published in association with Extraordinary Wellness™; Christmas Tree Ranch, LLC, 2833 Crockett St., Suite 158, Fort Worth, TX 76107

ISBN: 979-8-89292-323-1; Book Format: Paperback; Nov. 2023; $14.99

Some names and details have been changed in a few real-life stories to protect the privacy of the individuals involved. All stories have been told with permission.

All resources referenced or provided in the book or listed at the back of the book, come from public domains and are accessible to the general public. We neither endorse, or are endorsed by any of the resources, organizations, or professionals mentioned, or provided by any of the contributors in this publication.

Acknowledgment

Content Creators & Our Support System

Thank you, thank you, and thank you! A heartfelt acknowledgment goes to my Code Grape Tribe for their swift involvement in bringing this miraculous project to completion. From the authors and curators to those interviewed, this endeavor unfolded with a speed, precision, and preciousness that can only be attributed to divine intervention.

We want to honor the women that have made permanent imprints on our lives through the years. Thank you for choosing us, and for taking time to invest in us!

We want to bless and honor the women we have walked along side with both support and accountability, you have made our lives richer, and we are better your presence!

We want to recognize the amazing husbands, children, nieces & nephews, Kingdom siblings, aunts & uncles, moms & dads, granny's & papa's, and more, that have been a part of our support system and stood in the gap when other's that should have been support were not available to us. Thank you for being the hands and feet of Christ to assist us in our journey!

And a special thank you to the women who allowed us to feature their journeys and stories! Your lives inspire us to remember who we were created to be! Your real authentic human selves, redeemed by Christ, and presented in raw form help us make sense of our own worlds. They offer insights and possibilities, pose challenges and express sorrow, along with offering wisdom and resources to navigate this unpredictable crisis we call life!

This book is dedicated to our dear friend

-.˙ ★ *Careman Williams* ★ ˙.-

Careman spent her life dedicated to Cross-Cultural Kingdom work! Her final work was in the service of developing important warning systems for the people living in the Himalayas. Throughout her life, she has helped hundreds of thousands of others with lifesaving interventions. Moreover, she has disciplined countless numbers of disciples. She will be missed by the living, but we know she is having the best "kitchen dance party" with our Savior! She will forever be my favorite prison buddy and a personal hero!

Careman understood that God wired us to know and be known, to love and be loved, to serve and be served, and to celebrate and be celebrated.

Careman demonstrated love through her actions, and we were fortunate to have her in our lives!

Table of Contents

We're a basic group of God-centric sisters sharing magnificent stories of the ordinary women, mentors, and tribes, with extraordinary approaches to their journeys...

Code Grape hopes to
bring a little peace,
laughter, wisdom, and support
to this amazing Crisis Event we call life!

Chapter One

We Believe

"The Lord gives the command; the women who proclaim the good news are a GREAT army."
~Psalm 68:11

WE BELIEVE God designed you on purpose and created you with innate value.

WE BELIEVE you are a person of value who has been called to see value in others!

WE BELIEVE that you have been set apart to gain tools to add value to the lives of others!

To do this well, we need to be 'well' ourselves. With the remarkable progress in contemporary medicine, therapy, and technology, one might expect that we would all experience the utmost satisfaction, peace, and overall well-being in the history of humanity.

Unfortunately, what we find are high rates of depression, anxiety, and burnout, and that's across the board from children to elderly, from business gurus to wellness workers, from ministers to medical professionals, from teachers to truck drivers!

If you are converting oxygen into carbon dioxide, it means you are alive. We are convinced that God has designated you as an individual of immense worth! He has given us support within the social context called His Church, and the Church is made up of people.

"Let's Do This!": Selling a house and planning a move can be an excruciating experience. It's a great test of your patience barometer, that's for sure! My husband Fitz and I were listing our house in Crowley, Texas, and had some last-minute things to finish up before realtor photos were to be taken on Monday. I had an amazing tribe come together to help get the space ready, seriously, by the time Holly and Dannette were done, I didn't want to move… it was too fabulous! I told my hubby we were buying our own house back… it didn't fly, but it was worth a try! Thank you both for making our house look so much more amazing than it actually was! Side note: if you ever need staging or photos to make a space sell, I've got your team!

Ok, so there I was, with an eight and a six-year-old running around the house playing with our puppy Sampson, while I was determined to nail up the last of the crown molding... in three rooms. Did I mention Fitz was out of town for work? I'm just saying.

I could tell that at this rate, it would take me at least 5 to 6 hours, but I was decided! And although I was psyched up to get it done, I could tell I was losing time and strength. I decided to 'phone a friend' for advice and knew that if anyone knew a better method or hack, my friend Mercy would be my information lifeline... Mercy happens to be the owner of a small construction company. That's right, yes, SHE does! I simply asked her if she had a more effective solution, to which she quickly replied, "I can be there in 20 minutes, trust me, you need my nail guns!"

So, in my mind and with a big smile forming on my face, I'm thinking, "That sounded amazing" and I'm imagining myself like a super elegant Charlie's Angel with a double-handed hold on a nail gun pointed in the air, in a sassy pose, and a cool holster of course! Then, within a split-second, I jolted back to reality, talk about whiplash from being double-minded, and my emotions and face completely changed. I thought to myself, "Oh man, I don't know anything about construction equipment. I hope it's not complicated. I don't want to disappoint Mercy or break her cool tools! And, what if it's too difficult or heavy to use?" At that moment, I'm totally imagining myself falling off the ladder, cartoon style, both hands on the nail gun trigger with 'nail bullets' spraying everywhere! And the kids and Sampson in full sprint, duck and cover fashion to the other rooms in fear! Seriously, it took longer to share what went through my mind, than it did in real-time. For some reason, the next thing I heard come out of my mouth was, "That sounds great! See you soon!" and I knew Mercy was on her way!

Now remember, Mercy said nail 'guns,' honestly, I didn't even think twice about the plural 's' at the end of that word when she said it. That is until Mercy walks in, with what I can only explain as an 'arsenal' of nail guns. Seriously, my cousin Mark is a legitimate gun collector, but my construction friend Mercy might have the corner market on nail gun options, all sizes and colors - don't judge! In a stunning sequined gold dress, Mercy walks up like the Nigerian

African Queen she is, with gorgeous intricately braided hair, flawless make-up, stunning nails, and fabulous shoes. And with TWO rolling suitcases, she cascades right into my dining room. She gives me a huge hug and simply says, "I don't have a lot of time, but I have all the firepower you need. Let's do this!" I told her I thought she was a bit overdressed for the crown molding occasion, to which she responded, "Nonsense, sequins are always a good idea, not to mention you used the word 'crown' in the details!"

Remember, I'm doing repairs around the house. I'm in a paint-splattered t-shirt, messy mom ponytail, and 80's-version jean-material overalls. Not to mention, I have been working all day to get the house ready for market next Monday! Yet, my natural reply is, "You are so right girl, we've got this!" No doubt her confidence in the "do-ability" of the situation evoked confidence in me, too! She begins saying words that I don't really understand, but I fully trust her, this is Mercy's world!

Now, I have had the privilege of participating in some pretty interesting and fabulous covert operations and intriguing diplomacy work around the world, but the way Mercy nonchalantly opened her two cases of power tools was smooth. She began pulling out power-move options the same way I would pull out a laptop and lip-gloss when getting ready for an important meeting. It was impressive. Then, she casually says, "You need a lightweight high-powered pneumatic." "Of course," I responded with a slight head nod. With a very mater-of-fact look, she asks, "Do you want a bounce-fire trigger or a sequential trigger?" And in comedian 'Shane Smith' style I said, "You KNOW what I want!" Mainly because I had no clue, and I knew that she would actually know what I needed! Mercy goes back out to her truck and brings in a second ladder, still in heels! Then, she confidently placed one of these weapons in my hands, and after a 10-second YouTube-style lesson, we went to work! It's mind-blowing how having someone who had the right equipment and knew what they were doing, made it comparatively effortless to accomplish a previously perceived daunting task!

We finished ALL crown molding in about 45 minutes, no joke... "Take that, hammer and nails! Oh crown-molding, where is your sting now?!" It was a Christmas miracle in June! It looked amazing, with no splinters, no nail wounds, and we felt like Pinky and the Brain, prepared to take over the world! And the best part is that Mercy even had enough time to sit, braid some purple into my eight-year-old's hair, and finish a cup of tea before heading to her gala!

Needless to say, I learned several things that day. I thought about the struggle I had to hold the board and hammer the nail at the same time. I thought about how much energy it took to hammer even one nail, compared to the energy it took to pull a simple, lightweight trigger. I then started to think about how that compares to the Holy Spirit in our lives.

Could you imagine if we would stop laboring so hard to do things of our own understanding and power, things that I dare say we were never designed to do, much less by ourselves? What if we simply understood that the Holy Spirit has all the 'high-caliber power' needed to accomplish ALL things? Quick shout-out to Phil 4:13 that confirms this.

What if, instead of trying to fight the exhausting battle of the weight of the world, the negative self-talk, the broken heart, the cancer diagnosis, the ongoing disappointments, the depression, the divorce, the loss of loved ones, income, control, or opportunities? What if we realized that the power of the Holy Spirit, might be like the concept of power coming from a high-caliber gun? That is... what if the only energy required from me was a light trigger pull? Simply lifting a finger would access the power needed to accomplish a task?!

Truth... He has all the power, all the ability, and all the force needed! I don't need to do more. In fact, I need to put down the hammer that I keep bringing to the gunfight and simply do what I was created to do. I need to remember to worship my Creator and choose joyous satisfaction in that He can. Then, learn to pull the trigger, and step into the Power of His Spirit that is loaded and ready to go!

Remember the opening scripture that refers to an army of women? Imagine the force of an extraordinary God through ordinary women simply willing to use the ordinary power of a trigger finger to make extraordinary impacts for Kingdom causes! What if we partnered well with Kingdom Siblings? From Mercy's mouth to our ears, "Let's do this!"

We believe God gives us the ability to recognize, to become, and to seek out a sphere of support.

We all feel the stress of living in a high-speed, tech-driven society, with information at our fingertips & urgent expectations at every turn. We live in a world where the concept of 'connection' and belonging are often determined and blurred within the 'communities' we call social media. When we step back, we can actually see the source of these 'communities', which are made of mere plastic, metal, technology, and anonymity. And, if we're not careful, we can equate this with human relationships. Our emotions are so readily tied and swayed by what comes up on the screen and the truth is, tech is just a tool! Don't let social media give you emotional whiplash! Tech and media can both be used for good, for bad, with indifference, or worse, with little to no thought of the repercussions to follow. But, if we step back, social media is not the social context we want to use to determine our emotional state. We need better tools to manage our attitudes and emotions. We need a live tribe of other women who are in the Word, to have faith when we don't, to remind us of our value, simply because God said it was so, and to join us in our commissioning of impacting and adding value to others in our spheres of influence. Tech can be an equally brilliant or brutal tool, but remember, just as the people in our sphere are the ones who help us make sense of the world around us, we are in desperate need of a God who sets the standard and has established our value.

We get to recognize the value of other humans in our lives, as we walk alongside each other in this life, in the traumatic, in the terrible, and in the terrific! We believe nothing can replace the value of celebrations with other humans and with our living God, Jehovah!

CODE GRAPE! refers to cultivating a support system for crisis intervention in our everyday lives! It's an intentional choice to be vulnerable with others, to lean into relationships with others willing to do the same, to be Jesus with skin on, to be honest, and to be available. Choose people who have a record of being trustworthy to go to the Word for wisdom. Please remember, these are not perfect people, they are real humans who are making the same commitment as you. That means that it might get messy, but that forgiveness, love, and grace are the usual order of your relationship.

This particular book is showcasing and examining the lives and tribes of women who see the great value and true wellness in living intentionally, and intentionally surrounding themselves with other seemingly ordinary women they can walk alongside to experience moments of extraordinary wellness!

We believe God doesn't just want you to survive, but to thrive! We believe He wants you to step into extraordinary wellness and use your sphere of influence to bring wellness to others along your way!

He has set you apart for the mission of engaging well in your sphere! We believe He has intended us to live with a sound mind, and the spirit of peace, and to bring wellness and discipleship to those around us. It's important to think about the responsibility of that... The truth is that when we are not well ourselves, we can easily shift into becoming a liability of exasperating traumas, versus the desired outcome of bringing healing and wellness.

Side Note: If you haven't read *When Helping Hurts by Steve Corbett,* it's worth a read. It's about when we launch missionary but might not consider or be aware of those moments, actions, and thought patterns that reveal we have a personal agenda. We might be more of a discipleship-liability, in the name of good, instead of actually being a good Kingdom sibling.

The flight attendant cliché of placing the oxygen mask on yourself before others is critically important... it's not 'self-care' for selfish reasons. It's caring for self, so you can effectively step into your calling, and impact your sphere of influence as God intended! If you have found your salvation and identity in Jesus Christ, then you believe you are no longer a slave to fear, depression, or the world around you.

No longer being a "slave" to something doesn't mean you won't encounter traumas and hard things, but when you do encounter them, it means you can do so with the profound knowledge that you are a Child of God, with all of the access, accolade, and endowments that the title "Child of God" comes with. With that said, you and I both know that having the title or even the 'status' is not the same thing as stepping into the rightful authority and believing it in a moment or circumstance. This is why, at Extraordinary Wellness, we believe in the concept of the 4R Cycle: Rest, Rejuvenation, Revive, and Relaunch, which is critically important. We also believe walking in healing, wellness, peace, and competence is phenomenally more 'doable' when you call "Code Grape!" and access the God of the universe and the ***Tribe*** He has placed in your world! This is just one of the benefits that come with the heritage of being a child of God who has been rescued through His perfect love! To know more about what it means to be a child of God, please see the **'Well**(ness), **What's Next?'** section.

If you're reading this book, you might actually be interested in living a life of Extraordinary Wellness! We highly encourage you to connect with others to create or even develop further your own version of a Code Grape support system! It's refreshing and great to hear that so many are verbalizing and interested in achieving Extraordinary Wellness! We want to share with you a few helpful tools, a few spectacular stories, a few magnificent organizations, a few laughs at our own expense and humanity, as well as a few practical steps to walk alongside you and your Code Grape Tribe on this journey!

We, ourselves, are a small tribe of ordinary women, who love God most, our families and spheres of influence second, and seek to build a culture of extraordinary wellness together. We are honored and delighted that you have chosen to spend time hearing about some amazing women who are a part of our Code Grape Culture! We would LOVE to hear about God's presence and provision in the brilliant and brutal life stories you and yours are willing to share!

Please go to www.CODEGrape.org for more resources and to share your stories!

What is Code Grape?

Code Grape

... or is that *Aubergine?*

(Clairee Belcher – Steel Magnolias 1989)

"SO... A teacher, a cancer patient, and a missionary walk into a Smart-Barre..."

It sounds like the start of a bad dad-joke, but it's a great start to recognizing your Code Grape Tribe! Think about the women in your world, those important "doing life with" sisters who are in your sphere of influence!

Imagine yourself in an ER, and you hear, "Code Blue!" All around you, individuals in different uniforms jump into action as if they had rehearsed this exact moment for a Broadway production. It's truly amazing to watch as they communicate with each other in simple expectation of the exact role each of them is to perform next. It is intended to literally save lives.

Hospitals use color codes to convey essential information quickly, to jump into action while minimizing stress and panic. In fact, since 2000, the standardized trend to adopt emergency codes has continued to increase because of the effectiveness of communicating a problem and the most effective strategies to begin to address the problem. Most anyone who has ever been in a hospital or even watched TV for that matter has heard "Code Blue!", "Code Red!" or even "Code Black!" The combination of standardizing and adopting color codes has been used to increase the reaction time of successful trauma intervention. Technically, there's no formal definition for a "Code," but doctors often use the term as slang for situations like cardiopulmonary arrest happening to a patient, requiring a team of providers (sometimes called a "code team") to rush to the specific location and begin immediate resuscitative efforts. Wouldn't it be great if we, our tribe of friends, family, and Church used a similar tool?

Wait... it gets even better... **CODE Lavender** is a peer-crisis intervention tool used by medical communities to support coworkers and persons in their hospital or medical systems. Code Lavender includes the entire hospital sphere, from doctors and nurses who experience daily trauma to the patients, EMTs, volunteers, and other practitioners who are a part of the system. They come together to create an intentionally available community, equipped with basic trauma-intervention and listening tools. They have access to resources so that when, not if, but **when** there is a difficult, traumatic moment encountered, you have a simple process, and you don't have to survive it alone!

Code Grape is our version of a daily LIFE crisis intervention concept to support Kingdom Builders and their sphere of influence. The name Code Grape is patterned on the Code Lavender concept, but the color 'grape' is taken from the sister-reviewed support system of "Steel Magnolias," a great movie gift to tribes of women, salons, and back porches everywhere!

Code Grape is truly for any woman converting oxygen into carbon dioxide who wants to intentionally build their tribe of support. These are the women that you gather into your life that are there as a 'phone a friend,' 'grab a cup of coffee,' or the women you regularly 'bend a knee with.' These are the very 'lifelines' that help you deal with the complexities of life and community! Code Grape Tribes are ideal for the teacher who needs a growth mindset, or for the behavior specialist who needs help dealing with their own teen's struggling behavior, or the missionary struggling with a secret sin, or the nurse who needs support while walking through her own cancer diagnosis.

The goal is to be in a position relationally to both give and receive support when it is needed.

- To be in a position to receive or to speak into someone's life.

- To recognize and participate in the value of Speaking Peace, Life, Wisdom, and Authority into and over other Wonder Women Warriors.
- These are the mamas and Mijas... the wives, sistas, aunties, and executives... the first responders, non-profit workers, and counselors... the philanthropists, ministers, and grandmothers... the professionals, the teachers, and the next-door neighbors in your sphere of influence, these are YOUR Code Grape girls... Your tribe!

In this book, we want to share with you some of the women and wisdom in our extended Code Grape Tribes. Whether you have a seasoned Code Grape group you 'do life with' or you're seeking to develop your own tribe of trusted Code Grape sisters, we want to bring you a starter set of magnificent stories from ours. We are real women with real stories, which are simply straight dedicated to the game of life, seeking to grow in extraordinary wellness together, and at minimum, keep showing up for each other! We hope to bring a little laughter, wisdom, and support to this amazing Crisis Event we call Life!

Segments Covered in this Book:

- "If you're trying to drive me crazy, it's too late!"
  ~ **Themes** of life

- "I'm Over 40 & I Know Some Stuff Now!"
  ~ **Chats** with the Specialists in their Fields

- "Well Done Good & Faithful"
  ~ **Spotlights** on Organizations *"Doing it well!"*

- "Bless Your Heart"
  ~ **Faux Pas',** stories, quotes, comments, and some often well-meaning, but unfortunately embarrassing, humorous, or tactless actions or remarks in a social situation. *Go ahead and laugh, because we all have them!*

- "Gods Got You, We'll Walk with You, You've Got This!"
  ~ **Practical Applications:** Tools, devotions, journals, and prayers to help you tap into your privilege as a child of God, use your gorgeous guidebook we call the Bible, step into your trusted Code Grape Tribe, and experience Extraordinary Wellness.

EXTRAORDINARY WELLNESS

4R - REST || REJUVENATE || REVIVE || RELAUNCH

The concept of Extraordinary Wellness is a 4R cycle to keep us in a progression of wellness: Rest, Rejuvenate, Revive, and Relaunch! The 4Rs come from a collaboration of men and women across every walk of life and culture worldwide, beginning with the wisdom of Gospel commands of rest, joy, discipleship, and commissioning. As a team of practitioners, we then read and reviewed established research and conducted our own surveys and interviews with a series of professionals, practitioners, and patients. We started exploring vicarious trauma and burnout rates among teachers, counselors, ministers, as well as medical workers, and other first responders. From there, we gathered surveys from behavioral specialists, neuroscientists, prayer warriors, ministers, business owners, veterans, students, terminally ill patients, trauma survivors, and medical practitioners coming together to approach wellness with a holistic approach addressing Body, Mind, and Spirit wellness through a Biblical worldview.

The four foundational principles of Rest, Rejuvenate, Revive, and to Relaunch, help us cycle through life's most precarious circumstances. These are detailed, defined, and discussed in the next few pages.

<u>REST // REJUVENATE // REVIVE // RELAUNCH</u>

// 1 REST //

syn **Disconnect, Peace (Reset)**

1. For Extraordinary Wellness purposes, **we define REST as disconnecting,** i.e., *taking a break from technology, responsibility, and people or circumstances that vie for your attention.* Intentionally setting aside focused attention to other usual distractions, needs, or schedules.

2. **Why?** *It's a healthy reset.* And, interestingly enough, it was one of the first practices commanded and modeled for us by God himself.

SPECTACULAR SABBATH: God, the most innovative creator in history, the creator of creators, designed, crafted, and artistically sculpted the universe, the stunning globe we call home. Genesis 2:2-3 tells us that He created the seas, the heavens, even the magnificent living creatures sharing the earth with us, and so on... and THEN on the seventh day He rested! He rested? Wait, what? I mean, I'm pretty exhausted thinking about all of that creative planning, wielding, and building, but God is God! God doesn't need rest! Right? So, the only logical conclusion this feeble brain can conjure is that He intentionally modeled one-seventh of His week to rest, solely for the vulnerable humans, that He adores and even made in his likeness. The very creatures who would be reading His Word. Plain and simple, WE need rest. God knew. And God was gracious enough to make sure we saw it, heard it, and understood we would need to make it a priority! Exodus 20:8-10 gets super clear on the expectations of rest. As a species, especially in our fast-paced lives, too often rest is what you do when you have leftover time. My mama always told me that if you don't plan your time, someone or something else will take it from you! Come to think of it, it might be her fault that I am a 'plan to make a plan' person! Thanks, Mom.

3. Looking for a different outlet to Rest?

    1. **Take time off...** schedule an entire hour or better yet, a day, that you are without your phone! I know, the very thought just made someone's heart stop, but it is one of the most liberating things we can do to help remove the 'yoke' of being a slave to impulse connection. A regular 15-30min, tech-free break, where you can stop, breathe deep, and savor something... anything really. Savor a favorite cup of coffee, or tea, perhaps a favorite verse, or a piece of chocolate.

       Chocolate Kisses: When Annie and I lived in Kenya, that's a story for another time, my break from the crazy chaos, was to step outside, and have a chocolate kiss! As long as the kiss was still melting in my mouth, I was on break mentally, emotionally, and fully disconnected from the responsibilities around me. I knew the calls, requirements, schedules, and needs would resume after the kiss had melted away, but for about 3 minutes, I was free! I knew I would return shortly and could re-engage with the worry and stress when I was done. And I actually let my body, mind, and spirit settle into the break, into a state of Rest. I was much younger, I had just turned 30, and honestly, I don't think I even realized how healthy that moment of 'chocolate-savoring' was, I just knew that when I didn't take my 'kiss break' I wasn't quite as patient or gentle or conscientious of other's needs. I also knew other people could tell the difference, even if they didn't know what caused the difference. I'm convinced that chocolate is good for you because of that very reason! Go ahead, change my mind!

2. **Plan, plan, and plan!** Proverbs 29:18 tells us that "for lack of a plan, My people parish" … I don't think it's much of a stretch for the word 'parish' to be synonymous with "become exhausted!"

   I'm one of those annoying planners who will plan to make a plan! I know that drives normal people crazy, but honestly, for me, it gives my brain a place and space to rest. I know I now have time set aside to intentionally focus on "that thing" whatever it is, at a later time. It's the same marriage concept of "plan your fight," and schedule a time for you and your spouse to discuss a disagreement instead of in the heat of the moment. This provides breathing room and time to reset and prepare. Both of us can take time to find calm, rational ways to communicate our "side" and it helps to avoid the instinct to be offended, defensive or to throw accusations. And for the planners, we know that we're coming back to it at the scheduled time, so we don't have to dwell on it now; we'll deal with it when the appointed time comes. For my husband Jonathan, we have to make it a quick turnaround or the waiting could cause him anxiety, so we try not to go past the 24-hour mark. Sometimes that works great and sometimes not so much, but it's a great tool to try and it has probably saved our marriage on more than a few occasions! Pray for Jonathan, praise God he's an amazing, patient, and kind man! He is legitimately the 'good one' in this relationship! And, if you're not familiar with Fight Night by Les and Leslie Parot, it's highly recommended!

Make it a practice to intentionally schedule rest. Plan a random day off every 6 months to simply sleep in! Do it monthly, if possible! If you need to be in a different location, go to a hotel, or phone a friend and ask to borrow an empty room for the night or day! Sleep and getting enough is crucial for your physical and mental well-being. In fact, doctors, and those who play doctors on TV, recommend 7-9 hours of sleep per night1.

Meditate: Take time in nature or kneel in quiet meditative reverence before God.

// 2 REJUVENATION //

syn **Enjoyment, Laughter (Regulate)**

1. For Extraordinary Wellness purposes, **we define Rejuvenation as a healthy experience that you would describe as fun, joyful,** or one that might cause your face to crack, in a good way, you know, into a smile of course.

   What does rejuvenation look like? Simply, it is the expression of **enjoyment, laughing, smiling, letting your hair down**, or **breathing deep with satisfaction!**

2. **Why?** It's a healthy way to regulate! **This is your body's physical reaction to regulating itself!** The physical action of a smile or laugh can change your brain chemistry! Hearing a familiar song and singing along can trigger your body chemistry and completely change your mood!

   If you haven't stumbled upon Dr. Caroline Leaf, I highly recommend reading, 'Switch on Your Brain: The Key to Peak Happiness.' Her podcasts are life-changing and her book 'Think and Eat Yourself Smart' was brilliant. She's worth a Google search. She's the kind of person I would LOVE to have in my Code Grape tribe!

   Joy & laughter are critically important to the 4R Cycle, in fact, according to Proverbs 17:22, Laughter is to the soul, like acetaminophen is to headaches!

3. Looking for a different Rejuvenation outlet?

    1. Consider taking a break from your daily routine and going on a wellness retreat. Wellness retreats offer a variety of activities such as yoga, meditation, and spa treatments that can help you relax and rejuvenate.

    2. Pull up your favorite comedy sketches on YouTube or even check out Dry Bar comedy.

    3. Take time to kitchen dance or sing… you know what we're talking about! Turn the fun and fabulous music up, sing out loud, and dance like you mean it!

Kitchen Dancing: My brilliant, beautiful niece Princess, yes, that's her real name, and I would make a regular practice of kitchen dancing. That's right, we would sing and dance so loud and so hard, that our pet Shizu wasn't sure if we were having fun or needed help! What Cessa didn't know then is that those moments were needed to help us regulate, increase endorphins, and get our head in the game to start, or end, our day right… especially when we had big emotions to deal with or needed to bring them under control.

// 3 REVIVE //

syn **Equipping, Wisdom (Growth Mindset)**

1. For Extraordinary Wellness purposes, **we define Revive as growth and being equipped with new tools** through a rested and rejuvenated lens. Be revived through knowledge and seek wisdom from the Creator Himself. It is taking the time to learn new practices through new or 'revisited' content. It's being able to gain valuable tools after resetting, which can help you stay mentally sharp and improve your overall well-being.

2. **Why?** Revival is a sign of healthy growth. The Bible has so much to say about knowledge and learning. Let's just start with **Proverbs 18:15** which tells us that an "intelligent heart acquires knowledge, and the ear of the wise seeks knowledge." And **Proverbs 1:7** says, "The fear of the Lord is the beginning of knowledge; fools despise wisdom and instruction." Don't be a fool... when you're given corrective criticism, take it gladly, with a grain of salt if needed, but lean in and see if God has some nuggets of knowledge for you to hear!

3. **Looking for a different outlet to Revive?**

    1. Consider taking an online course or attending a workshop on a topic that interests you.

2. This is the time to learn that second language you've always talked about. You know, the one you purchased online a couple of years ago. Don't judge; I know I'm not the only one!

   This is the perfect time to read that book, listen to that podcast, or start that Bible study with your tribe, hubby, or kiddos. Learning together, in a community, is a truly precious experience!

// 4 RELAUNCH //

syn **Engage, Support (Value Sphere of Influence)**

1. For Extraordinary Wellness purposes, **we define RELAUNCH as stepping into life or ministry with a refreshed mind… re-engaging successfully into your sphere of influence.** Once you've rested, rejuvenated, and learned something through a new perspective, it's time to put your newfound mindset, energy, and knowledge to use!

2. **Why?** Relaunching is the fruit of healthy living and healthy ministry. Many of you reading **this book will** be the ones who live the majority of your life in the 'Launching' phase of the 4R cycle, but we don't believe that is the healthiest practice. A favorite mentor of mine, Dr. Blackaby, says, "The truth is that God can do anything He pleases through an ordinary person who is fully dedicated to Him." That's me! I'm an ordinary person who serves an extraordinary God. Dr. Blackaby further talks about joining God in His work, instead of simply making our own paths, and asking God to bless them. It's funny how narcissistic we can actually be and yet still call it "ministry." Praise God, He is a gracious and merciful God who actually steps in to forgive, heal, grow and then allow us to join Him! Sometimes, it's important to get to the prayer, "Lord, I've made a mess of my life, it's yours if you want it!" And the best part is that Jehovah Yahweh will take us up on that offer every time! And He can use ordinary humans with surrender and obedience to accomplish His extraordinary will! Mind-blowing!

I'll leave you with this one last Dr. Blackaby'ism,

"You cannot stay where you are and go with God."

Research shows that to have a healthy impact on our sphere of influence, we have to spend intentional and quality time in peace, joy, and growth. To neglect any one of these can be detrimental to everyone around you, including yourself. A basic Biblical principle throughout the scripture is wellness. We are instructed to "be well", so we can "impact well" so that "others can model after the wellness!" 1 Tim 3:5 is one of Paul's letters to the Church and is dedicated to honest dialogue about getting our own houses in order before reorganizing other people's homes! Paul poses a great question, "If you don't take care of your own house, how can you take care of others in His Church?"

Furthermore, Jesus tells us in John that the world will know who God is by the way **we,** His disciples, love one another... so, here's another question: how well are we actually loving the Church? In fact, I want to take a minute and ponder that, especially regarding our personal lives and the larger context of making disciples.

3. Looking for a different outlet to Relaunch?

    1. Remember that ministry, and launching well is less about 'doing more or for,' and more about 'walking with' those in your sphere of influence!

2. Think about where you currently spend most of your time. Who is there? Who needs to experience love through you? Is there an opportunity to intercede? The answer is yes... we can, at any moment, in any space, choose to walk in the Power of the Holy Spirit to intentionally bless and pour into those in our sphere of influence. Is there a way to do it differently than you previously have?

3. Consider volunteering in your community or joining a group near you that aligns with your interests.

4. Imagine yourself in the environment of your work or ministry, how can you apply the newfound tools or wisdom gained during your Revive stage? Is there a way to love and minister more effectively, yet with less wear and tear on your physical body or emotional well-being?

REST WELL |
Rethinking a Biblical Approach to Rest

In this section, we are engaging with stories, journeys, and content through the lens of **RESTING** well. Extraordinary Wellness uses the following acronym to help us understand, plan for, and apply REST in our daily lives.

ReST | Scripture Hebrews 4:9-11

"There remains, then, a Sabbath-rest for the people of God; for anyone who enters God's rest also rests from their works, just as God did from his.

Let us, therefore, make every effort to enter that rest, so that no one will perish by following their example of disobedience."

Definition: Disconnect; Reset //

We define REST as disconnecting or taking a break from technology, responsibility, and people or circumstances that vie for your attention.

Strategically set aside the time and attention that is usually dedicated to the 'everyday' and 'other' needs, distractions, or schedules.

- **Rethinking Rest |** A restful approach to defining Extraordinary Wellness Body, Mind & Soul; Unplugging from Personal Technology, and connection with your Creator (worship, prayer, scripture reading). The goal is to have a mental, emotional, and physical break to help us 'reset.'

- **Set aside Time |** Calendar rest. Really think about this and make it a priority. Choose a date ahead of time, put it on your calendar, and look forward to it. Choose to have slow intentional movement.

- **Territorial Support |** Restful Environmental Support. This means a place or location of Physical Safety, Mental Safety, Emotional Safety, and Spiritual Safety. A place you can have a 'Calgon' moment, and 'let your hair down.' This could be far away in the mountains or near the ocean, it could be in your closet, in a park, in a library, at a friend's house, or even in a hot bubble bath. Anywhere that is 'away' and allows you time to be in an isolated refuge mentally and emotionally. Tip: Being in nature, with no connected technology, has a way of helping us breathe deep and reset.

Create a *Culture of Rest*

Culture can be described as the characteristic features of everyday existence (such as diversions or a way of life), usually shared by people in a common place or time. This means making rest an everyday practice in small moments and scheduling and setting aside larger amounts of time in the future to rest. Both are important practices that we see Jesus model for us in the Scripture. How can you create space in your regular routine to rest? What could this look like for you?

Make *Rest Culture* a Practice

- Pull in your Code Grape Tribe and brainstorm together. Get intentional about making Biblical Rest a NORM and a feature of your everyday existence.

- Lean into your Code Grape Tribe for accountability and support.

- The Father has commanded us to REST!

- Use all five senses to help you disconnect and rest. How could you use your senses to work for you as you rest and regulate?

- Breathe deep and do the work of 'releasing work' when it's time to rest!

If You're Trying to Drive Me Crazy, It's Too Late!

Real Stories, Real Woman, Real Themes of Life
By: Aimee Rhodes

We are here to tell you **REST** is achievable in all the true stories you are about to read! **There is hope!**

Single, Professional Woman

Kendra is a 37-year-old single professional woman who should feel like she has a good life and all the time to rest, yet she feels so disjointed and honestly leaves her job each day thinking, "If you're trying to drive me crazy, it's too late".

She works in the community health sector and has high expectations for herself, as does her boss. Her hard work gets rewarded with even more work. You see, Kendra carries a caseload of 30 clients and just was handed five more at the end of her day. She sees her clients weekly and wants to do what is right for them but often can't seem to get her own life in order. She tells her clients to use their time off to care for themselves, but Kendra hasn't taken time off in 3 years.

She commutes to her job at least 45 minutes each way and keeps late appointments because she feels like she needs to martyr herself for the cause of those in need. She quietly thinks to herself, "I feel so busy and cannot take on one more thing, but I am struggling with being alone". She sighs and then mutters under her breath, "My job is seeing clients all day with emotional needs and even medical needs. The weight of the world falls on my shoulders, day in and day out. I am lucky if I get two days pressed together to do all the normal upkeep around my home".

Her mind wanders to the things she can do to maybe circumvent the added pressures of her role. "Do I get this dog, or do I throw myself into online dating yet again? I don't go to bars or clubs... I always feel like an outsider... my friends are married or married with children". Her mind wanders to images of her as another misfit toy on the island with all the other misfit toys. She quickly snaps back to reality and mutters, "I have some friends, but honestly, these days, their lives are so full of drama; I just can't take any more of it. I wake up and just have to pull myself together and go through the motions, cause nobody else will pay my bills."

Kendra dreams of taking time off and often thinks, "If I keep going, surely, I will feel like I can get over the hurdle of just wanting to curl under a blanket and sleep the day away." She finds herself feeling crispy around the edges, and on edge when she shows up to work, and it never seems to go away. Yet, she keeps pushing herself despite having nothing left for herself.

A single professional woman's heart cry for rest is usually a result of a filled schedule, and stressors of work, friends, and even family. She longs for the connection but is inundated with the emotional toll of her job, navigating relationships, whether she would fight for what she wants or perhaps take on a pet for companionship. Her emotional capacity is tapped out and honestly, it just feels like one more thing will break her. Avoiding the next straw to break the camel's back will require intention. She is sure if she sees one more wedding announcement or more cases added to her to-do list, this indeed just might drive her crazy.

Living with Chronic Illness/Terminal Illnesses

Maya, a 46-year-old married woman with no kids, has always been riddled with life's issues from a very young age. She has fought doctors to get properly diagnosed, and no one, and I mean no one knows how infuriating it is except Maya to be told: "You're fine. It's all in your head." Maya has seen 10 different doctors throughout her lifetime, trying to navigate this myriad of symptoms that just don't add up. Maya eats a clean diet; she gets regular cardio and occasionally lifts weights. She, however, is fatigued; can't move around as much and just feels pain throughout her body no matter what she does.

She often feels like she can't retrieve the words she is looking for. And when she can find the word, it comes out as "salsa". She feverishly busies herself partly to distract herself from the physical symptoms but also because she loves what she does. She is creative and loves how her work connects with others and helps them shine too. You see, Maya, pushes herself in all the ways but often is frustrated because she doesn't know how to disconnect from the constant demands of trying to figure out how to help her body and finding a doctor who will finally listen to the fact that she is suffering in silence.

People pass her on the street saying, "Oh she looks fine," when Maya wishes it was only a cup of coffee that could deliver the energy and focus that she desperately needs. Maya loves coffee too, but certainly knows it just isn't going to cut it. Maya reminisces to herself, thinking "Was there ever a time I didn't feel this way? I miss my old self. I feel like I've aged 100 years these last few years. I cannot think straight, my words come out jumbled". She slowly thinks to herself, "If I keep at this rate, I am going to have to just give up". Maya picks herself up and sets up yet another doctor's appointment, waiting and waiting for answers.

Time passes, and she attends her appointment. The doctor reviews her lab work with her explaining yet a few more issues they find in her blood work. She now has high white cell counts in her urine, leaving the doctors stumped as to what is going on in her body. Maya sighs with a subtle thought, "If you are trying to drive me crazy, it's too late!". Maya pours over the lab results thinking... "What is it now? Could someone just tell me what is wrong with me?" Maya has become increasingly anxious about attending further doctor's appointments because, "What is the point? They can't seem to figure it out". She is whisked out of the office with a referral and sent on her way. She was just tired of dealing with all the symptoms and was pretty sure it was only going to keep getting worse. Maya took the day off just to be told, "We can't help you..." and now she's off to see a specialist.

She begrudgingly schedules a follow-up appointment with the specialist because she is done. She is so done with all the lack of answers, disappointment and fueling herself to just mask the pain, the confusion, and the hurt she feels. Her husband is kind and caring but has no real answers either. He just prays that this specialist will be able to give some answers and help Maya figure out what is going on for her because Maya becomes so dejected from her experiences with the medical world leading to depressive isolation. **Maya just wishes** she had the energy to spend time with her husband, her friends, a night out, or even do the basic tasks at work and home.

Mamahood, from Littles to Hormonal Teenagers

Fatima, a mama of three with one on the way, divides her time between her children, juggling appointments, time with her husband, and the pets her children somehow brought home. They have adopted, from rabbits to kittens and a family dog too. Fatima laughs hesitantly as she recalls that she doesn't have a moment alone. Quite literally she often wonders if she is made of Velcro because her children are attached to her at all times. They are on her lap in the bathroom while she tries to pee, or have followed her into the shower, and are sitting on her lap during mealtime.

Fatima's mental health is stretched thin as she tries to figure out if wiping the sleep out of her eyes counts as self-care. She smiles and thinks how much she adores and loves her children... but then comes the argument. Her children let out a blood-curdling scream and Fatima flinches, closing her eyes before taking a deep breath. She hears shouts of 'Mom! Mommy! Mama!' as she walks into the living room attempting to pull her children apart and ascertain what happened, helping her kids to regulate their emotions and stop blaming one another.

Fatima's husband is supportive and helpful with the children but works outside the home, so Fatima is home alone with three children under the age of four. Fatima pauses and closes her eyes, thinking to herself, "It won't always be like this". She tries to take that idea and push forward.

She meets with her friend, whose children are all teenagers and full of hormones, navigating the gap of life between childhood and adulthood. Fatima's friend shares the same complaints of feeling there is not enough time, juggling schedules, worrying about what their children are doing with their friends, what they are consuming on the internet, and whether they are being good humans to other kids their age. Both women think to themselves if their children are trying to drive them crazy with their choices... They both struggle and sigh about their children's antics, fights and often joke, "It's too late, I'm already crazy!"

Fatima is desperate for space, and most importantly, rest. She isn't sure how she can get it but recognizes the need as she also faces the idea of going back to work even part-time. **She wonders** how she is ever going to do this. How can she carve out time when there is quite literally no more time?

Living Life with Older Parents in Late Stages of Life

Charlene, in her early 50s, has a pretty balanced life on the surface. She has a good job, decent health, and is married with a couple of kids who have turned out to be some of her favorite people. Charlene's parents live close by in their own home. Her parents, when they retired, moved closer to be near their grandchildren. Charlene and her husband spend one concentrated day with her parents and one day with his parents. Both sets of parents are older and in their late 70s and early 80s. They have each had multiple surgeries: a back, a knee, both hips, and, not to mention dealing with high blood pressure, insulin-dependent diabetes, and the crippling depression that has settled over them because their peers are dying off one by one.

Charlene's parents are dependent upon her to bring groceries as they don't get out as much. Driving to the store and shopping would be far too much for them physically. They tried to do grocery pick up but just don't trust technology as much as the younger generations. Charlene has started to notice both her parents' memories are beginning to fail and worries because their recall of whether they have even taken their medication isn't there.

Charlene walked into the parent's home and found her parents had fallen off their beds or chairs at various times, and they didn't call for help. Charlene attempts to help her parents interact with family and friends, but they refuse to let people come visit. She rolls her eyes and grinds her teeth, wondering if they are truly trying to make her crazy or if this is just the stage of life her parents are in. Charlene has attempted to support her parents through the use of timers, calendars, med reminders, and spending time reminiscing. Over time, she has noticed more and more of her mother looking at her with a deer-in-the-headlight look, as if she doesn't recognize her. Charlene knows, her parents aren't driving her crazy. She knows it's time to make hard decisions to support them in this end stage of life.

She ponders, what is best for their family. "Should I clean out our extra recreation room, move my parents in, and sell my parents' house?" She hesitantly asks her husband. He listens quietly and considers it. He throws out ideas of senior retirement villages or possible assisted living facilities. Her husband, while open to the idea, is also worried about his parents needing care too.

Charlene puts her face into her hands, letting out a sigh of stress. She has forgotten to take a deep breath and feels the tension arising between them and within herself. She truly thinks she is at the end of her rope and all she can take on with caring for her parents. "How can I care for them in my home when the demand is only getting worse?" In the same breath, she says to herself, "How can I let them live in one of those places? Nobody can care for my family the same way I can." Charlene knows she is feeling fatigued as a caregiver for her aging parents and knows the demands will only get worse if this really is dementia setting in for them.

The restless stories of these women are all too often experienced in our own lives.

We are giving 110% of ourselves and have nothing left at the end of the day. They are tired, constantly busy, and connected to their problems, glued to their phones, just waiting for the other shoe to drop.

They feel like they are also scrolling social media as a means to be available to everyone at all times. They see the latest war-torn news, the plights of their friends, and the political divide of those they love. Their minds and their hearts are tired. They want true rest. But they are quickly reminded of the adage there is no rest for the weary, or you can sleep when you are dead.

We are here to confirm... **Rest is achievable** in all these circumstances.

There is hope.

I'm Over 40 and I Know Some Stuff Now!

Chats with Specialists in their Fields.

Yolanda Fraser

Vulnerable Embarrassment

Counselor, Social Worker, Disciple, Minister, Wife & Mom

Grieving... it's not usually a term you hear synonymous with REST. Yolanda has taught us to think differently about grieving and rest. Yolanda and I have been working on a Parent University project, and the topic of grieving has come up on several occasions. One of the things Yolanda said was, "Grieving interrupts everything, and it is different and unique for everyone, but one thing doesn't change, it is important to prioritize rest while coping with grief so that we can begin to engage with the grief." I'm so thankful to my dear friend Yolanda who teaches us to be vulnerable and to grieve losses, of any kind, in our lives.

~ TLC

To be honest, sometimes I'm not very mindful of caring for my own health as I am blinded by the legitimate needs of others. I am learning the art of delegation, and it has literally saved my life. In 2016, I suffered a stroke that left my speech impaired, and the right side of my body with limited mobility. It was evident as I struggled to walk and to grasp. I was devastated as I walked into this Rehabilitation Center where I would attend therapy for 90 days. I started at 09:00 AM and worked until 03:30 PM. I received speech, occupational, and physical therapy. I was embarrassed. I had an undiagnosed sleep disorder that led to this brain injury. How could I not have known? Why was I not a better steward of my body and my time?

During my journey of recovery, I learned the joy of saying, "no", delegating, and not embracing the role of "strong woman." My greatest coping strategy that helped me to improve my boundaries is what I call the "intentional delayed response." I have always been quick to respond or to settle a matter, but I began gathering my thoughts, acknowledging God, and allowing him to direct my paths. When asked a specific request, I now ask for a few minutes, a few hours, or a few days before I answer. This may seem basic to others, but it has allowed me to hear that still-small voice or call a friend/mentor for counsel. God fully restored my health, and I am so grateful.

As I walked with my physical therapist during my rehabilitation, I asked the Lord to recover me as I dedicated my life to recovering others. I serve out of a place of rest, not might. Now, my greatest role is being His daughter.

Kate Jordan

<u>Brittle, Dry, & Crusty!</u>
Non-Profit Leadership,
Grants, & Global Endeavors

Talk about Code Grape and jumping into action! My Kate is definitely one of those amazing tribal warriors for me that can jump into action when needed. It was summer 2021. My kiddos were going to Kenya for the summer, and I'll spare you the backstory, but I promised AJ, I would be there to pick him up and bring him back home. Just trust me, I ***needed*** *to be there. I had been diagnosed with cancer again, pesky cancer, and they put me on a new medicine, two weeks before I was supposed to leave, which caused my memory and thought process to be a bit shaky, to say the least. I knew I had to go, so, I called Kate! "Hey, what are you doing for the next two weeks? Any chance you can go to Kenya with me next Monday?!" To which she replied, "Let me call my boss and talk him into it! Can I let you know tomorrow?!" And she came with me, making it possible for me to fulfill some very important commitments! Who does that?! Code Grape Kate does that! Friends, THAT is a literal example of Code Grape! Jumping into action! I'm forever grateful!*

~ TLC

For me, time to unwind might look like Angry Birds and an audiobook or podcast. It might look like digging my fingers in the dirt of my garden. Or it might look like time with my people. My grown kids. My parents. And chosen family who have poured love into me and upon whom I have also loved, many for decades now. The key is unplugging from stressors and seeking the things that fuel me rather than drain away my energy. That's when I'm your everyday, garden variety kind of tired.

But there is another kind of tiredness. It's the soul-deep exhaustion of having run on fumes for too long. Having burned the candle at both ends until the stub left in the middle is perilously small.

Having served a few years on the mission field, living cross-culturally in a Muslim country, I poured out and out and out until I felt like a dried-up sponge. Brittle, dry, crusty, and with nothing left to give. I felt like all the resources I once had in abundance were drained away, and in their place, there was... nothing. Emptiness. A yawning void. The Bible says, "My cup runneth over," but mine had run completely dry.

I needed rest! I needed self-care. I needed time to worship freely and openly. I needed time in scripture. I had just managed a trans-Atlantic move for a family of five, left a people and a place I had come to deeply love, and bought a house sight-unseen where we were camping out while we awaited the arrival of our household goods, which were somewhere in the middle of the ocean, slowly steaming toward the East Coast.

Meanwhile, I had three kids who were transitioning back to life in American public schools and finding that the sweet kids they had gone to elementary school with had grown up in a lot of ways that weren't so easy for them to understand. I had a husband who was trying to find a new identity and new employment after first serving in the military and then on the mission field. And I was dealing with my own reassimilation into the land of plenty after being somewhere that was totally "other." To make a long story short, I had a lot on my plate, and nothing left in the tank.

I was overextended and overwrought in every sense of both words. Yet when my family returned to our local fellowship, it was like a feeding frenzy! I heard from Women's Ministry - would I lead a weekly Bible study? I heard from the Children's Ministry, could I help with Sunday School? I heard from the Missions pastor, would I consider crafting a framework for global missions and service projects? I heard from the local Mothers of Preschoolers group; would I be a mentor for young mothers? The Young Adult Ministry my husband and I had previously co-led also came calling. They were in a leadership transition, and would we consider stepping back in?

I thought my head was going to explode!

So, I did it. I did that thing that is so hard for those of us who were raised in the South to do.

I said, "No."

To all of it.

And in saying no to all the "good" things that were asked of me, I was able to say, "Yes" to the important things. My children. My home. My own need for time and restoration.

I started meeting weekly with a very small group of five women who were in ministry, pouring out and feeling that same brittleness. We worked through some Bible study books, but more importantly, we prayed together. We shared what was happening in our lives. We walked alongside one another and shared our struggles, our sorrows, and our joys. Those women, that Tribe, buoyed me up. They poured into me. Slowly, I didn't feel so dried up and depleted anymore. I was encouraged. I was cared for. I knew I wasn't alone.

It took more than a year. A year of **solitude**. But I emerged from that dry and weary land into a green place. A fertile place. A place where I could serve again. Where I was ready to take on responsibilities again and do it with joy.

So, sweet sister, I'll leave you with this. If you're worn out and bowed down, it's OK to say "No." It's OK to take time for yourself, to place the oxygen mask over your own nose and mouth before you assist others. There are times we have to say "No" so that we can be prepared to say "Yes!" There is new life waiting on the other side!

Well Done Good & Faithful

Spotlights on Organizations & Groups "Doing it well!"

While most companies and organizations focus on faster, bigger, better, and more... these organizations or executive individuals have found the brilliance, beauty, and 'better' through **REST**. Some have learned to practice resting well, while some are teaching or training the practice of rest to achieve their organization's mission statement.

"Rest is a weapon given to us by God. The enemy hates it because he wants you to be stressed and occupied."

~ Elizabeth Elliot

Jesus said, "Come to me . . . and I will give you rest."

~ Matt 11:28

What an incredible invitation from God himself, if you really think about it... that sounds amazing! Interestingly enough, just before that spectacular invitation, according to Luke 11:46, He was rebuking leaders for 'stealing rest.' "You load people with burdens hard to bear, and you yourselves do not touch the burdens with one of your fingers."

NOTE: The Following Interview is a special one requiring a few changes for protection and security purposes. Please note that all interviews are conducted with real sisters who are precious and important to us and for Kingdom purposes!

Global Catalytic Ministries

~ Ann Lindholm

Director of Special Operations
www.catalyticministries.com

Mission: GCM aims to transform Muslims in the Middle East and around the world through leadership development, church planting, & compassion ministries.

What a gift Ann and her team are! They're probably more of a gift to the Church than most people will ever have the opportunity to fully understand! That they are often 'unseen' is what makes them so strategic and powerful! This is not an organization that you would naturally align with REST, but through the course of her interview, you can hear the powerful and important tool REST has become.

I loved getting to know her phenomenal background in anti-terrorism and intelligence. It's rare to find someone who shares a similar path of strategic Global Operations and its alignment with Global Missions. The hand of the Lord on her life is unmistakable. Ann's organization has been a strategic partner in helping many Global Teams of Kingdom builders.

It is because GCM operates strategically with integrity, intelligence, and Kingdom-minded stewardship, that many other Cross-Culture Christians can accomplish the work God called them to… in places and spaces of terror across the world!

~ TLC

Interview Content with Ann Lindholm

I have been operating in Global Security and Logistics and crisis management for over three years with a previous 10+ year history in counter-terrorism. I took a seven-year hiatus to homeschool my children. Working in counter-terrorism with a focus on Islamic threats, more specifically the Muslim Brotherhood (in political arm of Islam), my heart grew hard towards the Muslim community.

About ten years ago, God began breaking and softening my heart for these very precious people. I divinely stumbled across the documentary "Sheep Among Wolves" on YouTube in November of 2019. I vividly recall falling to my knees and weeping for the Middle East. I knew in my heart I was called there.

When Afghanistan fell to the Taliban in August of 2021, another colleague reached out for help with organizing emergency evacuations of persecuted people and American citizens. Volunteering 100% of my time, often 16–24-hour days for six weeks, I found myself deeply entrenched in a whole new world…a world that uniquely involved discipleship in ways I had never imagined. That is until I recalled the day I saw 'Sheep Among Wolves.' It was then that God took me on a journey back into my past thirty years, and he began to reveal to me how he had been preparing me for such a time as this. Little did I know just how strategically he had placed me over the years.

I quickly discovered the importance and value of relationships and networking. I received a call from the point person on our team asking me if I was interested in a job. This was the beginning of the next phase of my life. My children were almost all grown up and moving on. I was now a single, empty nester turning the page to a new chapter, both personally, and spiritually. I attended Tarrant County College while I was single and pregnant with my first daughter. I was majoring in Psychology. I had to postpone my education to work full-time. I went back to school online in 2005, changing my major to Counter Terrorism and Homeland Security. I also found myself very deeply involved in politics and briefing legislators, and local enforcement and schools on the Islamic threat of the Muslim Brotherhood.

I did not complete my schooling as I had three more children and began focusing on parenting and homeschooling. I have received numerous other certifications in counter terrorism, homeland security, counterintelligence, spy craft, investigative research, trauma-informed care, crisis management; kidnap, hostage, ransom negotiations; global security, cultural awareness, and more. I am a Christian. I'm not aligned with any denomination or sect. I just follow God's Word.

My faith has greatly impacted my work in many miraculous ways. My faith is what drives the heart behind all I do. Because of my line of work and the people I work with, I am strategically positioned to minister and disciple those in very distressed circumstances. I have had the privilege of discipling Muslims, colleagues, and even sponsors. There are numerous accounts where my faith and prayer supernaturally guided us to save lives and walk in such discernment that we changed our path of action, resulting in successful missions. I was married for twenty years and recently went through a divorce. We have four children. Unlike many divorces, we actually get along very well and continue to co-parent.

Being a woman in a leadership position as a mom is challenging. But add to that the intense field in which I work, it gets extremely challenging. One of the most difficult things I struggle with is balancing my personal time away from work, mainly due to the dynamics of my job. Much of the work I do takes place on the other side of the globe. So, there are time zone differences. Additionally, this work is not an 8-5 kind of job. Our work is dictated by terrorist organizations, evil regimes, hostile groups, etc. We cannot predict when they are going to hunt down someone on the kill list or go chasing after Christians or Hazaras. When someone is on the run for their life and a call comes in, I cannot really ask them to wait while I finish my dinner. So, needless to say…time management…well actually, I am really good at prioritizing tasks when it comes to work, maybe just not personally. Expecting my children to understand that a sexually assaulted mom, because of her faith who is running from the Taliban, takes precedence is very difficult. They cannot be expected to comprehend this. And yet, this poor woman cannot wait for me to take the time to explain this to my children. How does one make such a decision? It reminds me of the scenes during Hurricane Katrina when a mom had to make the devastating choice to hold on to one of her babies or let go of that one to rescue the other one drowning in the rushing waters. Overall, though, I must commend my children for being understanding, compassionate, patient, and so merciful. Global Catalytic Ministries (GCM) focuses on discipleship in the 10/40 Window and beyond. In the past few years, we have been seeing what works in the East is effective in the West, it just takes a lot longer.

The organization approaches discipleship from a biblical perspective, focusing on facilitating or hoisting a conversation between the person and God. We merely introduce them to God through the Word and lead them on a path of discovery. We share stories with them from the Bible and ask them exploratory questions that lead them on a path of knowing God personally and deconstructing any previous wrong teachings or beliefs. Additionally, we lead them to obedience to the Word based on scripture. This obedience includes discipling them to disciple others. We are not church planters. We are disciple-makers, who make disciple-makers, then a church (God's people who assemble together for Biblical community) organically grows from these groups that naturally form out of the discovery of Bible studies.

When it comes to wellness, GCM has stewarded this very well. Ironically, we have come from a very difficult season as an organization, and I personally have come through a challenging few years. Rest, rejuvenation, revive, and to relaunch are crucial parts of our overall health as a team. Thankfully, we have amazing leaders who are forging the path in this regard. We have multiple team meetings a month via technology, and as leaders, we are all very good at going to our team members and investing in personal time with people. Overall, when we have opportunities to meet in person, we make it happen. During these visits, both online and in person, we always encourage one another to take time to rest in the presence of Adonai.

In fact, "Rest" has been a theme we have felt God impressing upon our hearts in this season. Discipleship is no light matter. It is difficult, tiring, heartbreaking, and time-consuming. Many of us are in this full-time. Much like the cycle of changing seasons, in order to revive, the seed must experience death, before it can produce new fruit. So, we too, must die to the old things and let them fall away before we can experience new growth. While in this season, it may feel painful or sad, but there is so much liberation, beauty, and fruit on the other side.

Rejuvenation goes along with rest and revive and marries into relaunching. One cannot relaunch without having had a period of rest, rejuvenation, and revival.

At GCM, we yearn for this process as it was originated and designed by God himself. We can see it exhibited in all of his natural creations. Take a look at the life cycle of the butterfly, the entire circle of life, for that matter. Look at the human life cycle. Our organization encourages and fosters this approach to how we live and operate as a family and individually. We recognize that by failing to follow the blueprint God gave us, we will fail. We will fall short of attaining the prize. We will grow weary and not endure to the end. So, at GCM, we champion the process of resting, rejuvenating, reviving, and relaunching. I find it difficult to choose just one area to say that I am thriving in because I do not see them as individual things. I see them as a circular cycle that all fit together. With my line of work, sometimes it can feel like we do not have the opportunity to follow this cycle on a regular or consistent pattern. I have to be flexible. However, I will say, that I typically recognize when I need to step away from the phone and the incessant crises and pause.

Some of my favorite ways of doing this are stepping outside barefoot, walking on the ground, and feeling the warmth seep through the soles of my feet. I walk on the grass and the dirt and feel the earth massage my feet. I stand and stretch my arms out, tilt my head toward the sun, and feel the warmth of His fire kiss my skin. Feeling the breezes dance through my hair reminds me of how real and ever-present He is. I will lay on the concrete of the driveway or lay in the grass, soak in the rays, and just listen. I listen for the sounds around me. I listen for the sounds from heaven, from His voice. Sometimes, I cry out to Him and ask Him for help, guidance, or peace. He never fails to answer my pleas for His presence.

Other times, if it has been a terribly difficult day, I go to the local cemetery. It is rather large for our rural town. The trees throw incredibly bold colors in the fall and spring. I walk through the gravel roads, taking the somber, peacefulness of the graveyard. It may seem strange, but somehow walking around the cemetery, grounds me. It reminds me of how small I am and how short this life is. It reminds me how important it is to focus on the important, eternal things. It reminds me that no matter how important I think I am, I am not the Savior. I can only be a catalyst for discipling others to Him. As hard as it is to swallow, walking in the cemetery also reminds me that I need to have faith in God and his eternal promises, and that the death of the physical body is not the last stop. However, this also rejuvenates my desire and urgency to go and make disciples.

What are my hobbies and passions away from work?

I consider myself to be a disciple maker first and foremost. This is a lifestyle. It does not take a break. My work consists of discipleship and it's my passion to help others who are suffering. My job is 24/7 and is my hobby and passion. Not many people can say that about their work. I do not feel like I can call what I do, work. In addition to this, I do have other things I am passionate about.

Being outside gives me great pleasure. Gathering with others and sharing the love of God is one of my favorite places to be.

I love being around my children, and my family.

I also enjoy solitude, reading, studying, learning new languages, and just sitting and listening to God.

Exercising, and running feel good.

Traveling the world, learning about cultures, and making new lifelong friends truly bring me great joy and I pray that I can do this as long as I live on this earth.

The one area that I know I need to implement more is resting. Admittedly, it is very difficult for me to just sit and not do anything when I know there is so much suffering going on in the world. However, I tend to feel when I need to break away and rest. I am usually pretty good about starting my day off this way. I believe that I need to trust God during this time and put my phone and laptop in another room. Perhaps this is the nudge I needed.

Lit Bible Study

~ Chloe Love

Executive Director
www.litbiblestudy.com

Mission: Your Community For Fellowship And Growth In Christ.

It is such a special moment to introduce Chloe to this space. Chloe and I grew up together in our teen years as we attended high school together, served as Captains on our dance/drill team, and continued forward with college. Over the years, I have been able to watch how God has entrusted to her such a God-sized vision that was birthed through surrender and obedience. Chloe is such a raw gem in Jesus, and the group she is called to is one that is often underserved. Her willingness to open her home to hundreds of strangers and people over the process of her organization's growth is a grace in itself. Chloe continues to lead her team well through implementing times of rest and connection, and she truly values people. Chloe's sincere approach to Ministry is refreshing and so humbling. I am so honored to hear all that God is doing through Lit and Chloe's selfless leadership. I hope you enjoy and are encouraged by my dear friend, Chloe.

~ Amy

Interview Content with
Chloe Love

Share with us about the Ministry you help Steward:

Our leaders say LIT Bible Study began for one reason: it was the will of God. It took two years of prayer and discernment before meetups began, but once they did, the young millennials who started LIT never looked back.

LIT Bible Study originated at my house to serve those who wanted to continue studying throughout holiday breaks from Bible study at church. Once the first break was coming to an end, all attendees agreed that they wanted to continue meeting up every week. We have since grown from 12 to 150 meetings weekly, which required us to find another meeting space within 6-7 months, as we outgrew my living room and kitchen (people were sitting on my countertops and I had to think quickly!). What we learned in this season was that people enjoyed and felt most comfortable meeting somewhere where dialogue was encouraged, questions could be asked, godly friendships were built, and we weren't in an actual church building. Six years later, we still strive to keep this model and have made tweaks over the years to stay on top of what retains attendees and what helps people learn the Word best. We have grown into a dynamic 501c3 with multiple committees that our executive team leads, such as Finance, Fellowship, Communications, Curriculum, and Operations. We host frequent events to continue encouraging everyone to build relationships (which has also resulted in a few marriages over the years) and to have a community that holds each other accountable in their walk with Christ. We love relearning what it means to be a Christian as an adult, and we constantly encourage young adults to join us every week.

Tell us about your journey.

When I began LIT 6 years ago, I was dating but not yet married. The idea of LIT was placed in my heart 3 years prior in 2014, but God had me in the perfect position to start it in 2017. God took me through a pruning season for a couple of months before I realized I was going to start LIT. When I did, it required a lot of alone time and praying. I listened to what the Lord wanted me to do via the dreams I was having. This caused me to stay focused on what was to come, and that helped to make sure my earthly relationships were pure. As we prepared for marriage, my now husband was inspired to further build his relationship with God to be the spiritual leader that our household would need. He is very supportive in all ways necessary, and I couldn't ask for more. He has always been very inspired by me and my work in ministry with LIT, at my church, and in daily life. He believes meeting me allowed him to rebuild and deepen his own faith.

Which of the Extraordinary Wellness 4Rs, does your organization work to incorporate?

As an organization, I believe we implement rejuvenation very well. Whether that means taking a break from leading your team, adding a co-chair to assist the load, having fellowship nights with our executive team and individual teams to maintain bonds, praying together, regular wellness check-ins to make sure we can continue leading well, bringing new ideas to the table, and making sure we do not forget our purpose and privilege to serve.

Which of the 4Rs, do you intentionally incorporate practice in your life?

Personally, I think back to my introduction story. It was 'getting away' and intentionally stepping into the discipline of REST, that the Lord used to bring me to the place where I was able to obediently begin Lit. Implementing rest and rejuvenation is easiest for me because I live by my calendar and alarms, and I intentionally schedule time for myself and my family. Some of the activities that bring me joy. I also love to exercise. I always have some random new interest that is one day replaced by another random new interest. I love finding new places to eat, I love art in all forms, and I love spending time with my husband doing anything.

Bless Your Heart

Faux Pas' and embarrassing or tactless acts or remarks in the crazy social situations we find ourselves!

// Bless MeMaw's Heart //

|| By Shari Walker ||

Let me start with the fact that I have MS. I walk with a cane, my children joke that I look drunk when I walk, and my close friends with other diseases and I are rather cheeky and happy to have fun with our diseases, at our own expense. We know it's not politically correct, but it's our life and it's funny! Remember, joy is a choice! You work with what you've got! With that said, my MS does not define me… but apparently, for MeMaw, it does get to change my name! Bless MeMaw's heart!

When I was diagnosed with MS, I was not the only one who had to get their brain wrapped around a new reality. This became most apparent at a family reunion hosted by my grandmother. I was set to answer questions from close family members even though I really didn't have the answers. I could at least fake a positive attitude and confident outlook for an afternoon. I could even get ready for the tilted head sympathetic looks from aunts, uncles, and cousins.

What I wasn't prepared for was to be introduced to distant relatives by my grandmother as follows: "This is my granddaughter,

Shari. She has MS." I have to say, I felt a little like I had the scarlet letters M.S. stitched on my shirt. It took me by surprise the first couple of times, but once I realized this was my day, and it was going to be ok, I quickly found the humor and can look back on it with a smile. And for the rest of that day, my name was Shari with MS!

Bless her heart. My grandmother was dealing with my diagnosis the best she could. She didn't know what the future held any better than I did.

I just needed to give her the space and grace to process difficult news in her own way as well.

// Mom Mishaps //

|| By Emily Bryant ||

Nothing says rest and disconnect like a camping trip?!

My family was desperate for a reset. At the time, we were a family of 5, about 2 months shy of becoming 6! We adored caring for our 9-year-old son and our two daughters aged 7 and 4. Even though we only had a few days, my husband, James, and I were going to make it happen. We were craving sometime in God's country and needed some time to be away from our normal situation: an organized chaos that repeated itself daily until we felt like we were going to bust at the seams. Don't get me wrong. We love our babies, and we love caring for them. We were just weary. Getting out of town would enable us to slow down, UNPLUG, and enjoy being with God, each other, our kids, and nature.

The location was easy. We would visit my childhood favorite camping spot just a few hours away in the hill country of Texas. Numerous springs flow into different ice-cold swimming areas and would be the perfect retreat to a hot summer day in Texas. Between swimming, basking on rocks, rope swings, hiking, and exploring, we really could not ask for more in a camp-site or location. The springs also reminded me of my own childhood. My dad would lovingly take my sisters and me camping, and I remember feeling that adventure was around every bend-- not carefully planned and executed-- as so much of adulting can feel like sometimes.

Since I was expecting, what felt like any day now, and we had three children under the age of 10, we knew we had our work cut out for us. The days of camping in a tent with a fan had long passed, and we had learned this the hard way of course. To have an enjoyable camping trip at this stage, we knew we needed A/C and beds at a minimum. Electricity and water would also be a bonus. What could suit our needs better than a camper van?! We could pull it with my husband's truck, which would seat five for one last time.

Finding a 5th wheel or "camper van," as we called it, to rent was not difficult. A couple of Google searches and phone calls later, we had our home on wheels reserved. We were ecstatic. The kids were going to love it. The couch turned into a dining area, and the dining area further transformed into a bed. There was a bunk room, a master bedroom, a small kitchen, and even a bathroom! This was going to work. We had full confidence in our ability even though we were new to trailers. We had never rented a large camper before, but James owned a landscaping and irrigation business and was well-versed in driving and operating large vehicles and trailers. We were not new to camping, and not new to the driving aspect. We were golden.

Our adventure began at the trailer rental just outside of our hometown in Fort Worth, Texas. The owner gave us a quick run-through of the setup, the bells and whistles, and the takedown. James and the owner laughed and joked about this and that, and once we felt we understood everything, we hooked it up and went on our merry way. I was grateful to be married to someone who understood trailers, hitches, lights, and all the things that went into hauling one of these mammoths. It was also not beyond me that we had a vehicle powerful enough to pull it. My heart was grateful, hopeful, and excited that our growing family had this opportunity.

After stopping once an hour for my squished bladder, we finally made it to the hill country. The beautiful landscape welcomed us and gave us a renewed sense of energy and peace, and we were reminded of God's beauty and majesty. The children were able to run free, exploring their surroundings. We laughed and played, explored rocks, sat around campfires, and played family games. I couldn't stop taking pictures. It was our last trip before the baby, and I wanted to remember it forever!

Sunday came quickly as you might imagine. That morning, we noticed that the shower had stopped draining and that the gray water tank must be full. We had recently learned about these new terms: gray water was sink and shower water that had run into a tank under the camper, and black water was our toilet water droppings that three days and five people had accumulated. We had come prepared. The rental company provided us with a 20-foot hose to drain both tanks, and we had researched that this particular campsite needed a 15-foot hose to reach the proper receptacle. After packing everything up and loading everyone in the truck, we slowly drove the camper with the flooded shower over to the discharge area and opened the hatch that contained the hose. Much to our dismay, we opened the little door of the trailer to find a cute little 5-FOOT HOSE! Clearly, this was not going to work.

James painstakingly disconnected the truck from the trailer so that we could drive to the nearest gas station without sloshing shower water all over the camper. Inconvenient to be sure, but still do-able. We were informed that this particular gas station sold discharge hoses. GREAT!! We made it into the store to find out that they only sold those same cute little 5-footers. Seriously? Being that we needed 15 feet, we naturally bought 2 hoses to add to our existing one, which made a total of 15 feet. This was starting to look sketchy, but what choice did we have? We just needed to connect these guys.

Sadly, there were no couplers or other parts that would enable us to connect the hoses properly. We did, however, find a roll of duct tape. Problem solved! I'm pretty sure it's the go-to staple to fix all things! Ok, so it wasn't exactly our favorite choice, but again, we had to make something work here! And, it's duct tape, you would have done the same thing!

At this point, the kids were starting to get restless and whiny. We pumped them full of snacks and sugar, explaining that we were almost done with this little problem and would be on the road soon. Back at the campsite, James and I quickly began the process of connecting the hoses to the camper and taping the 5-foot pieces together. Oh yeah, this was shaping up nicely. It was definitely going to reach and work! The water did have to travel somewhat uphill, but that was what the pump was for. No big! We decided, being the novices that we were, that draining the gray water should come first since the shower was indeed overflowing.

James manned the pump and the switches, and I would stand in the middle of the hoses to ensure that they stayed together, and that water would continue flowing correctly. James switched it on, and the gray water began flowing out of the trailer into the receptacle. Our Jerry-rigged hose situation was working, and we were feeling genuinely accomplished. The shower was no longer flooded, and we had managed to keep the water from flowing onto the floor. WOOHOOOOO!! One down!

Next, James switched on the black water. Remember, this is a pee/poop concentrate from 5 people for 3 days. That's right, it was NOT going to smell great. As soon as he switched the black water on and we got a whiff, we began to rethink and regret the order of operations. Definitely should have drained the black water first!

Especially since the duct-taped joints were getting soggy from the gray water tank that had just flowed by minutes earlier.

As the black water flows slowly uphill, I notice that the duct tape joints are now legit saturated and beginning to drip. I try to position my hands so that the juice doesn't get onto my hands, but I fail. That's right, the drip turns into a small stream, and in that moment, at 8 months pregnant, I have finally reached the end of my rope. I scream, drop the hoses, letting sewage drip onto the ground.

I ran into the community bath house crying as if my life was over. Seriously, it wasn't pretty, there were tears, ugly faces, I was dry heaving, it was the whole package. All the while, James, God bless him, can't stop laughing at this sight and tries to finish the job. As I gather my composure, James attempts to "wash" the inside of the hose with a garden hose, only further exacerbating and spreading the sewage black water around the area. After all, we can't put a yucky hose back in the camper compartment!!! This became yet another ah-ha moment as to why one would want to 'finish with gray water' essentially rinsing out the inside of the discharge hose. It makes perfect sense on this side of the experience!

Even though our "restful camping retreat" turned on us, we definitely got joy and laughter, though for some of us, it was in hindsight! We loaded back up and headed for home with a great story, in need of rest from our rest retreat, never to use a camper since! As my friend once told me: when you play, you pay! This statement had never felt so true at that moment... but I wouldn't trade the memories with my family for one minute!

Praying for your restful family retreats to produce rest or joy in the journey! Even if joy becomes the only choice!

// It's True, I Heard it Once! //

|| By Ann Sullivan ||

Global Sticky Situations |
Interpol released Tonya, Yay! We can go play now!

I recently had the privilege of traveling with my friend, Tonya, who works with education, inter-cultural intelligence, and political intelligence agencies across the globe. While in the Kingdom of Jordan, Tonya and I were able to visit some friends and family. She wanted to make sure I had the opportunity to visit the Holy lands throughout Jordan and Israel, including Jerusalem, especially since it's only a couple hours of drive time from Amman to Jerusalem, not including the time for processing and visas at the international border of course. She also thought it would be a unique experience and perspective for me to see what it is like to travel across the militarized zone that separates Jordan and Israel. So, after a refreshing day relaxing at the Dead Sea, amazing, we began our initial stage of border crossing, from Jordan into Israel.

Honestly, everything was incredibly smooth and efficient, taking less than 2 hours. Come to find out that was record timing. Tonya and friends made sure that I was aware that this smooth and quick experience was unusual. In fact, it was without a seemingly single mishap, and we were ahead of schedule! We were going to have plenty of time to walk around Old City Jerusalem that evening and still get some much-needed rest to prepare for our tours to see all the sites!

After crossing over the Allenby Bridge to the Israeli checkpoint and completing our customs inspection, we met our taxi driver outside by the curb. This car service was new to Tonya but was recommended by an acquaintance who owns a travel agency, so she asked if we could give it a try as she is always looking for new partners for when she takes groups around the world. After a bit of confusion, the driver finally found us and promptly ushered the five of us into the vehicle with our luggage.

There were six of us getting into this vehicle, it wasn't exactly a van, but it did officially have a third row, so there's that. I crammed myself into the third row of seats with the luggage, just excited to be going to Jerusalem! Our driver, who resembled Professor Albert Einstein, had a wiry gray mustache and white hair that tufted out from under a ball cap. He whisked us away and around the bend we went. We were all excited to be on this enjoyable side trip before the work we had come to do began.

At this point, we had passed all the potential military concerns, so our guy friend in the front was getting to know our driver, and Tonya was in the middle seat buried in her phone, trying to confirm arrangements for Jerusalem while simultaneously working on arrangements for a refugee project in Asia coming up. Meanwhile, the rest of us are joyously and blindly riding along. Remember, we were fresh from the restful day at the Dead Sea, and so ready for this rejuvenating arrival in Old City Jerusalem. What is my life? This is amazing!

I realize that my description above made it sound simple and almost the equivalent of taking an Uber to the airport but, let me provide you with a short history lesson, one I didn't really take into account at the time, at least not fully… until I did.

Since the 1994 Israel-Jordan peace treaty, the Allenby Bridge Terminal has been operated by the Israel Authority. It serves as a border crossing between the west and east banks of the Jordan River. The bridge is currently the only official border crossing between the West Bank and Jordan and is the sole designated exit/entry point for West Bank Palestinians traveling abroad through the land. The Jordanian authorities recognize the bridge as an international border entry point, but neither Jordan nor Israel grant entry visas to foreign passport holders at this crossing. Three different political authorities are involved in this land crossing. All of whom are highly aware of the fragile peace that exists.

That's right... you heard me, Tonya, and friends were taking me through the "West Bank." Even when I first heard them say this, now especially AFTER having just crossed it, it comes with an awareness and a bit of a pause. But the experience seemed to be so smooth and not dissimilar from other land-border crossings of other countries. Remember, I've been to many sketchy places with Tonya, all of which had lots of guns. Come to think of it, I'm recognizing the common denominator here. I've digressed.

Anyway, to help you visualize, there are multiple checkpoints, many guards in military paraphernalia, and everyone has big black guns, they look serious, but even though it's a little intense crossing through this militarized area, all parties seemed in good spirits.

So, here we are in Israel, and the next thing we hear is a guard whistling and waving at us to pull over. Tonya looks up and says in a pretty serious voice, "That is a Jordanian sign, where are we?"

Then the guard comes over and proceeds to ask us if we are headed to Amman, Jordan. The driver and our friend in the front seat say, "No...we are headed to Jerusalem. We just got our visas for Israel."

Unbeknownst to us, after our driver picked us up, he took a wrong turn and promptly drove us back over the Allenby bridge across the border into Jordan. For those like me who have never traveled in this area of the world, I didn't realize what a HUGE faux pas this was until much later.

From the backseat, what I watched unfold felt like a scene from a movie. We were immediately directed to pull our car around while the armed guards spoke with our driver. In the blink of an eye, another vehicle promptly pulled in front of our vehicle and what looked a bit like a clown car poured out more IDF (Israeli Defense Force) soldiers than should have been humanly possible for that little car. What a scene.

And there I am, watching the awkward events unfold and giggling a bit from the back seat. I know. I know... I can't help it, all new to me - don't judge! God has given me a talent for finding joy in almost any situation, but especially when observing awkward interactions. I giggle, that's what I do!

The IDF began questioning our driver and then our crew. At that moment, our driver, who had a slight resemblance to a genius professor, started to speak, and we realized, oh, no, he's the absent-minded professor! Not the professor we were hoping for! Tonya was a bit quieter than usual, intently watching, listening, even texting... who could she be texting in a moment like this? But she was keenly aware of everything happening in the situation. The IDF gathered our passports and had us follow them back across the Allenby bridge for the THIRD time that day. Our driver nonchalantly followed behind their vehicle. There was a small bit of worry creeping in as the IDF now had ALL our passports, in a different vehicle driving away rather quickly. Once we arrived at the Israeli border, again, the IDF asked a few more questions but ultimately didn't see us as a threat, checked us in again, and then escorted us to the correct exit, making sure we were going out the correct gate leading to Jerusalem.

Unfortunately, as we pulled up to the exit, our absent-minded professor was ever-present... he could not find the blue ticket required to exit the checkpoint and enter Jerusalem. Seriously, this driver... Lord, help us! At this point, I think it's safe to say that Tonya will not be using this recommended driving service in the future... you win some, you lose some!

Yet again, we were forced to make another U-turn and reenter the Israeli checkpoint. While inside the checkpoint perimeter, our driver jumped out of the car and ran inside the facility to attempt to obtain the now lost but required exit pass. As the driver returned, we watched as our confused friend ran quickly, not to our vehicle, but mistakenly to someone else's vehicle anxiously thinking strangers were unloading his van. To leave the premises, we had to visit our IDF friends for a THIRD time.

The SAME officer that had just interrogated us about our dealings in the Palestinian territory, is the one who came over to us. He looked at us like we were crazy, "What are you doing back here?" Because of the multitude of bizarre behaviors of our driver, serious red flags were raised with our new IDF friends.

This time, they began asking more intense questions and took photo evidence of our vehicle and passports. Ultimately, they were allowed to pass into Jerusalem without too much further interrogation. However, because we crossed the militarized security checkpoints in Jordan, through the Palestinian nation Israel, officially three times in record time, my friend's diplomatic passport alerted Interpol and other authorities. So, fifteen minutes into our newfound freedom in Israel, on the open road to Jerusalem, one of Tonya's big bosses from France calls and begins asking her loads of questions about her whereabouts.

That's right, being triggered by Interpol for suspicious activity in the West Bank made for a fun conversation with Tonya's bosses. Remember, Tonya has some unique travels and experiences that come with her passport. This caused several groups to get involved. Tonya spent the next two days visiting a few State Departments, some UN authorities, and a few other entities, while the rest of us got to tour Jerusalem's Old City! She really didn't seem to mind, but in hindsight, I think she was just thankful that no one got arrested or detained longer than we did! We're still not sure about the entirety of what was discussed with Tonya behind those closed doors!

One thing I learned since the trip is that this crossing has a history of usage by smugglers who attempt to bring weapons into the West Bank. Our trip was in August of 2023, and after the events that unfolded in October of 2023, I now have a new perspective on the entire Middle East situation. I also have a better appreciation of the concerned authorities regarding our bizarre crossings. There is a unique benefit and comfort when traveling with a diplomat.

We eventually made it to Jerusalem, the Old City, Nazareth, and toured the Promised Land… and Praise the Lord, it was a magnificent trip. I'm thankful that sometimes He doesn't give us all the information, so we can experience His provision. I was traveling with highly skilled and connected individuals and though a bit apprehensive at different moments, I knew that unless Tonya told me to worry, it would be okay. She was serious and in her 'handle it mode,' but still in a calm demeanor. Luckily, we can all giggle about it now.

We definitely needed to rest and get a reset before taking in all the sites, but it was an experience I will never forget! Eventually, Tonya was squared with Interpol, and she was able to come join us for a few tours. In fact, I love how the Lord ultimately used that event and the diplomatic meetings it triggered, to cause Tonya to be in the right offices in Jerusalem, at the right time, to then open a door for our team to work freely in a closed Asian nation! Only God!

Talk about a God of redemption!

God's Got You
We'll Walk with You
You've Got This!

Practical Applications

Tools, devotions, journals, and prayers to help you tap into your privilege as a child of God, use your gorgeous guidebook, the Bible, step into your trusted Code Grape Tribe, and experience Extraordinary Wellness in your everyday!

// By: Natalyia Rutherford //

Whether it's our tech, our travels, our thoughts, those around us, or the responsibilities we find ourselves blessed with, we are called to disconnect from them and rest in our Father.

Jesus models this in Mark 1:35 - "And in the morning, rising up a great while before day, he went out, and departed into a solitary place, and there prayed." Not too much later, he has his disciples join his practice in Mark 6:31- "And he said to them, 'Come away by yourselves to a desolate place and rest a while.' For many were coming and going, and they had no leisure even to eat." I don't know about you, but I FEEL this! How many times have I been so busy parenting, working, serving, etc., that I forgot to eat??

Truly, Jesus gets us! He understands. Jesus experienced exhaustion and loneliness too. He's fully aware, we will too.

It's not that busyness for God's kingdom is wrong, It's that intimacy with Him is BEST. Our time with Him has to be first so that we can be fueled to do the work He has called us to.

Don't for a minute think that distractions aren't part of Satan's attack. It's small, it's subtle, but very effective. So, friend, take a minute to create a plan! We've broken down the most common distractions we all face into four categories to make them easier to tackle.

TECH

It's difficult to live these days without feeling the need to be connected at all times. Our work, our calendars, and our social life are tied to our laptops, phones, and even watches. Many of these devices have a digital wellness app now that can limit your scrolling (a total lifesaver for me). Some people have a family charging station, and everyone's devices are there during certain times of the day.

What boundaries can you set to keep these devices from distracting you?

___

___

___

___

___

How long should you keep these boundaries in place? Think through what is realistic for you. Will you need to revise these later? If so, go ahead and plan that now.

___

___

I John 5:21

"Dear children, keep away from anything that might take God's place in your hearts."

PEOPLE

People can hold so much power in our lives. Whether it's those we love or those that cause us pain, they can easily take up much of our mental space. We pray for them, we worry about them, we seek their approval. Though God created us to be relational, those around us can never fill the place He has reserved in our soul for Him.

How can you let go of the worries you have for those around you?

What are your go-to verses that remind you to seek approval from God first?

Psalm 62:1 "For God alone my soul waits in silence; from him comes my salvation."

RESPONSIBILITY So often the very things God has blessed us with can overtake our minds and therefore our energy... our families, our jobs, our sphere of influence, and even our calling or purpose. These are good things. If we didn't tend to them, God would have serious words for us! However, when we allow these good works to distract us from our time with Him, the impact can wreak havoc in our lives. Luke 10:38-42 tells the story of how Martha got so distracted by hosting/ serving Jesus that she forfeited time with him. None of us want that, but it can happen very easily.

How can you ensure the balance between the work God has called you to and creating time with Him?

____

____

____

____

____

Matt. 11:28 "Come to me all who are weary and heavy-laden, & I will give you rest for your souls."

THOUGHTS At times, we can be our own biggest distraction, more so than any of the above-mentioned. The expectations we set for ourselves, or worse, the expectations others put on us, play on repeat in our head. Those of us in ministry or service industries can especially struggle with this as EVERYTHING feels crucially important. What different choices would you make if you had permission to let go of these expectations?

Maybe your thoughts are filled with the painful, negative things you've been told and internalized. These voices can stay with us and create negative self-talk that crushes our spirit and guilts us into more activity. It's never enough.

There are times when the circumstances we find ourselves in take up every corner of our mind. Whether it's illness, finances, or some other major life change, the worries we have can be hard to let go of.

No matter where or how you find yourself struggling with these distractions, you are not alone. Take a few moments to fill each of the rays with a verse to help you battle in these times. Keeping His word on our hearts helps us release these worries and reminds us that He is in control.

Isaiah 26:3

(personalized for you!)

"You keep ___________ in perfect peace whose mind is stayed on you, because she trusts in you."

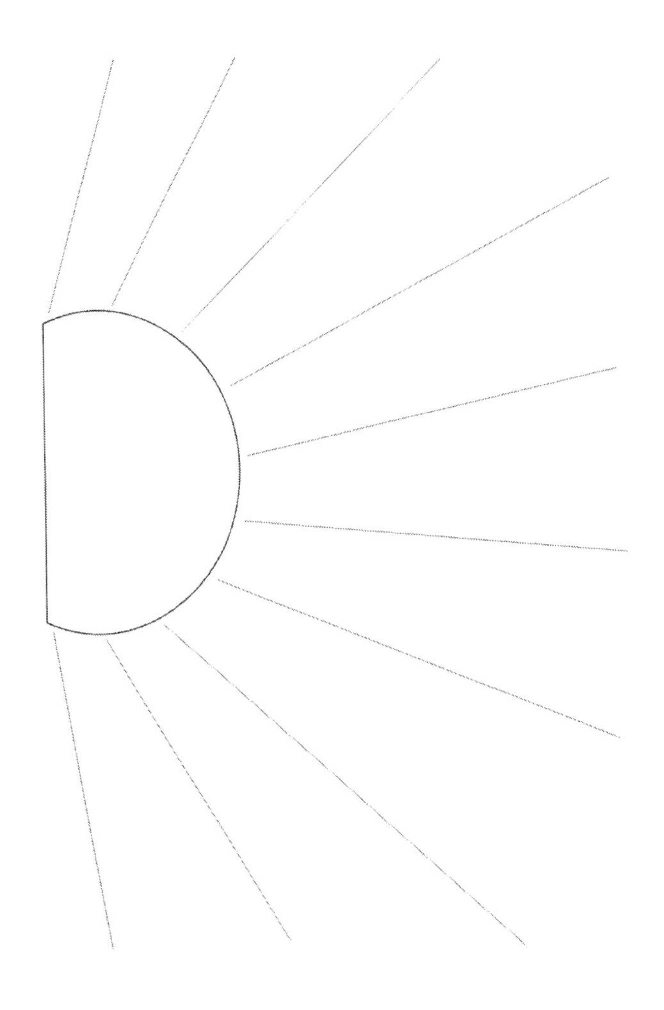

Hebrews 4:11

"Let us therefore strive to enter that rest, so that no one may fall by the same sort of disobedience."

God knows Satan's strategies. He knows distraction and exhaustion are two dangerous weapons Satan uses against us. Crafting a routine of rest in Him is not only our best defense but also our best offense as well. This isn't one more thing to add to your to-do list, THIS IS THE THING. Just as Solomon shared in Ecclesiastes, everything is meaningless when God is not at the center.

Paul also tells us in 1 Corinthians 13 that without love, his words and his works are nothing. So, friends, let's make a plan to rest in the One who is Love, the One who brings meaning to everything.

Let's start by recognizing signs of exhaustion. What are the early warning signs of burnout for you?

Great work! Now, let's craft a rest routine.

SPACES: Think about spaces where you can go to rest. Maybe it's stepping outside for 5 minutes, as Tonya shared, or maybe it's the end of the day at home and you have a little more time to practice rest.

TIME: I feel it's helpful to set aside time every day, but I also have an emergency plan for when I get overwhelmed and need a break. Really think through different scenarios you've been in. Is there a pattern? Maybe on your way to the school pick-up line? No? Just me?

REST What is the most helpful in these times? A lot of rest "practices" may depend on the spaces and times you've noted, but if there's one practice that really helps, you can build a time and space around that as well. I love Tonya's example of the chocolate kiss - it can be done anywhere when you don't have a lot of time. Some others include prayer walks, meditation (with yoga, yes please!), studying scripture, journaling, and deep breathing.

Now that you've thought it through, write it down!

Take a picture or save it somewhere quick and handy on your phone. You'll need to look back at it in those moments when you're too mentally drained and forgot to eat lunch!

My Rest Plan

PRAYER OF REST

Heavenly Father,

You are the author of the rest.

You created the heavens and the earth in six days, and on the seventh day, you rested. When you came to earth, you modeled rest and encouraged us to follow your perfect example. Lord, I confess that at times I become consumed with responsibilities. I become prideful, forgetting that You are the one who sustains me. Help me to step away from the bustle of the day to find rest in you. Thank you for leading me to a quiet place, beside still waters, where I can drink deeply from Your presence. Fill me with your Spirit. Draw me close to you, so I might find peace in your presence, and rest for my soul. Today, I pray that You establish these plans I've made to commit to rest.

Amen.

COME TO ME

By Jen Johnson; Bethel Music

Songwriters: Berry Gordy Jr, Marvin Earl Sr. Johnson.

This song is perhaps my favorite to get into a spiritual state of mind early in the morning, my readers should seriously Google and make it a part of their morning routine as well!

Chapter Three

Rejuvenate Culture

REJUVENATION |
Rethinking a Biblical Approach to Rejuvenation

In this section, we are discussing stories and knowledge through the lens of **REJUVENATING** well. Extraordinary Wellness uses the following acronym to help us understand, plan for, and apply REJUVENATION in our daily lives.

ReJUVENATION |

Scripture:
Nehemiah 8:10 (NIV)

"Go and enjoy choice food and sweet drinks, and send some to those who have nothing prepared. This day is holy

to our Lord. Do not grieve, for the joy of the LORD is your strength."

Definition: Enjoyment; Regulation

A healthy experience that you would describe as fun, joyful, or one that might cause your face to crack, in a good way, into a smile.

Rethinking Joy | Rejoicing is a Choice. Time in His Presence produces joy. Ask yourself, "what brings me joy?" Truth be told, we are all so unique that what brings me joy might bring others dread. Contemplate, "What brings my spouse or kids joy?" What similarities & distinctions do we share? How can I be intentional for each of us?

- **Stop,** and remember that **Joy is a Choice**.

- **Pause,** to connect with **my body**. If you're in nature, take time to use all five senses to appreciate the gift of life!

- **Pause,** to connect with **my God**. Take time to worship, praise, and listen in His presence.

JUVENile | Simplistic approach to Play and Community. Laughter, smirks, and giggles are always a good sign. These should be playful moments that could even get messy! Think about intentional movement and appreciation, from the tactile to the humorous. This could be engaging in an activity that is exhilarating or competitive... it could be contemplative, or in nature. Everything from sing-alongs and bad dad-jokes to creating or appreciating art, playing outside, and even playing instruments.

Actions | Brainstorm activities that bring joy to your day. It could be as simple as creating playlists for the car. Intentionally choose movements of joy such as dancing, exercise, yoga, competitive games (Pro Tip: Don't play Spoons with Lisa!), cooking, gardening, building, sculpting, painting, sunbathing, hot-tub, or the sauna @ my friend Nadia's house! If you can't find a sauna, just drive to Beaumont, Texas during June, July or Aug. Step out of the car... and breathe in the heat! The entire town is basically one huge, free sauna!

Treasured Moments | Make memories and treasure the moments at hand. Expect to enjoy, laugh, and have stories to tell others from these moments.

Intentional Celebrations | Celebrate the small things and give time to the people, activities, or experiences you haven't had time for or had to set on the back burner. (Ex: Celebrate the personal growth you have seen in your children, make new friends, celebrate the old ones, progress reports, host a costume party just because it makes you laugh, get thankful for God's gorgeous sunset, find brilliance and beauty in the little things)

Omnipotent | Resting my mind by making powerful, but simple declarations of God's sovereignty and the prize of Him being in control.

(Choose Joy by fixing your eyes on Jesus)

Nehemiah 8:10 | Meditate on the Joy of the Lord

- **Pause** to savor and enjoy small pleasures by utilizing each of our senses: tastes, smells, Kinetic sensory, and connection to the environment around us.

Remember the Chocolate kiss.

- Most of us have a favorite food, beverage, or essential oil.

- Some of us crave the peace and beauty of sunsets and ocean waves.

- Some can be transformed by the feel of a brisk breeze, massage, back scratch, water immersion, or even noticing the feel of different textures.

• **Host or attend a party…** sharing my joy and blessings in the context of community.

- For my **introverts** or quality time friends, call a friend or two for lunch or coffee!

Create a Culture of Rejuvenation

Remember, if culture is described as the characteristics of everyday existence (such as diversions or a way of life), usually shared by people in a common place or time, what does a Culture of Rejuvenation look like? Can you make healthy joy a daily priority? Can laughter be a regular practice? Can play be a regular practice? Is there a 'team' you can join?

Make Rejuvenation Culture a Practice

- Brainstorm people and places that bring you joy.
- Choose and engage in healthy activities that reduce stress and increase endorphins.
- What games or art delight your soul and give you a feeling of freedom or childlike well-being?

If You're Trying to Drive Me Crazy, It's Too Late!

Real Stories, Real Woman, Real Themes of Life
By: Aimee Rhodes

We are here to tell you **REJUVENATION** is achievable in all the true stories you are about to read! **There is hope!**

Single, Professional Woman

We revisited Kendra about 6 months later. Kendra finally took her first time off but still finds her life unfulfilling. She has tried every hobby in the book except the ones that actually work. She contemplates what life looks like from a place of enjoyment. She still is unsure of what it means to do self-care which she chuckles "I tell people to use self-care for a living! Why can't I seem to have self-care of my own?". That is the difference between teaching and doing, she thinks to herself. Kendra talks to her friends and her family, and they offer advice like "Take up running or have you tried yoga?". Kendra knows something has got to give because she forgets to eat and finds herself breathing shallowly most days.

She feels disconnected from what she loves. She sits at the edge of her chair, pausing, and says, "Heck, I don't even know what I love anymore. Her well-meaning friends have invited her to socialize at large, loud parties, while Kendra would be described as mild-mannered and soft-spoken. Kendra tries to attend these events and finds herself even more dysregulated and now notices her body feels like it's buzzing and electricity is all over her skin. She is uncomfortable and can't even sit still in her seat, even thinking about the sensation.

Kendra thinks one more advice session to try essential oils or soaking in a bath, while great for others, never really was her thing. Sitting in a bathtub with candles sounds like the worst idea to her. She prattles on about sitting in her own dirt, swirling around her. She sees no point in it. She exclaims, "Forget getting manicures or pedicures. That sounds like pure torture to me!". She feels crazy as all her friends swear by these options, but that isn't Kendra. Kendra knows there has to be something that will help her regulate but just doesn't know what her things are.

She doesn't know where to begin and feels a bit defeated about finding enjoyment in her community. Kendra dwells on the fact that she works late and wouldn't be able to enjoy anything anyway. She continues to put one foot in front of the other, day in and day out, feeling like this is her lot in life to just show up to work helping others, feeling crispy and almost resentful that she isn't enjoying things like she once did.

Living with Chronic Illness/Terminal Illnesses

Fast forward three months and we see Maya. She has seen the specialist finally and identified a couple of things that could be at play. The doctor reveals Maya has a rare autoimmune disease that has to be researched. The doctor also shared there was a huge mass that had been growing in her abdomen. Maya grows numb and cold. She quickly wants to lay in her bed in the fetal position because she is unsure how to process this news. She has lived with these symptoms for so long. She feels hurt, anger, and sadness. The feeling of powerlessness over her health just makes her want to give up. She feels like she has tried every diet in the book, except she keeps quitting midstream because it's unclear what to do, symptoms continue to persist, and she feels like her quality of life has gone downhill. She also finds herself feeling a sense of relief knowing what to call these symptoms. She still has yet another doctor's appointment to discuss treatment for the mass and to determine if this mass is indeed cancer and if anything can be done.

She's been isolated for some time, like everyone else, recovering from the trauma that was the pandemic. Two weeks turned into 3 years. She injured her ankle a month ago and just never rebounded to working out. It took the edge off for her but still wasn't providing that runner's high everyone claimed they got from it. She has resulted in her backup of watching copious amounts of TV shows that have taken her into a pattern of wash, rinse, and repeat. She doesn't really enjoy the shows but figures it's halfway better than scrolling on her phone day in and day out. She misses the days when she would do what she loves.

Now, she feels like it's just useless as many don't want to get her sick, but they are also dealing with their own lives. She wishes she had the energy to just do all the things again. Maya tries but finds her body fights back and typically wins, leaving her in bed for long periods of time and in a flare. "It's just not fair!" she screams as she can feel it in her joints that it's going to be one of those weeks.

Mamahood, from Littles to Hormonal Teenagers

We visited Fatima 6 months later in her home. She looks haphazardly dressed and like she hasn't been out of the house in months. Fatima is desperate for a break but also just had the baby 2 months ago and how important it is to bond. She still manages to juggle the other three children while nursing the new baby in the baby wrap close to her chest. She shares her mother-in-law is moving in to give Fatima a break, but Fatima thinks she might just take a nap instead of meeting up with her girlfriends.

Fatima longs for the days when she can get back to playing in the great outdoors without worrying her children will get lost in the woods or fall off a mountain. Fatima enjoyed rock climbing the most, along with camping, hiking, and slacklining with her husband. Fatima does not remember the last time she had gotten to do anything for herself that didn't have her children adhered to her side. Fatima loves all her children but is pretty sure they are trying to drive her crazy by bringing home another stray animal. She shares she feels like some days she's already crazy or barely hanging on by a thread.

Fatima breaks away only for a moment to put the sleepy newborn in his crib before she is tackled by her three other young children. She enjoys this moment but also wants to have an adult conversation that is not interrupted by her mom's duties. She hops on the phone to speak to her closest friend "Stop hitting your sister.... so how are you doing? Don't throw your shoes at the cat.... No, we cannot have another snack... so you were saying something about taking a new class?" She feels the tug of war happening to maintain some normalcy. While she gets to have decent conversations with her husband, sometimes it feels like they can only focus on the kids and less on their relationship. She just wants to have some enjoyment and fun again.

Fatima wonders when she will have enjoyment again that will allow her to disconnect from both the constant pace of the world's problems and maybe take a bit of a break from the kids, too. Cause she can't take one more shower with a kid attached to her leg.

Living Life with Older Parents in Late Stages of Life

Charlene, about 6 months ago, was making the very big decision of what to do with her parents with failing physical and mental health. She took her mother in for evaluations and found the very hard truth that indeed her mother has dementia setting in. Charlene was provided with some pamphlets from the doctor's office social worker and felt so defeated.

Charlene debates how to address dementia with the family as a whole but knows she has to start with the obvious by removing the driving privileges for her mom. She doesn't know how to break it to her parents that she is going to have to take away her mom's driver's license. Last month, her mother somehow made it to the store but forgot where she was. Charlene had to take off work just to go retrieve her from the security guard's office to ensure she got home safely. The store's managers and the security guard were worried if they let her mom leave, she might not make it back home. Thankfully, the store owners knew Charlene and the family from their local church and gave her a call. Charlene talks to her mom about driving to the store alone, and her mom bites back with harsh criticism that Charlene feels hurt but knows she needs to brush it off because that isn't who she knows her mom to be. She playfully bites back with "Are you trying to drive me crazy? Too late I already am". Her mother chuckles and says, "Me too!". They both laugh and cry a little cause they are both scared of the future.

Charlene decided to move her parents in with her and her husband's home so she could take on the caretaker role and have a closer eye on her parents' needs. Charlene took off work through her work resources for 6 months but quickly realized she was in over her head. She doesn't see friends often anymore, hasn't taken a pottery or painting class in some time, and has made it her job and mission to care for her father's physical and mother's needs. She steps outside for a breath of fresh air but buzzes around the home, caring for their every last need despite recently hiring a nurse who comes twice a week to help with their care needs. She feels like she is failing her parents but also has lost sight of what she enjoys. She doesn't know the last time she showered or slept more than 3-4 hours a night. She truly is exasperated by the demands of her parents but won't even take the break she can have when the nurse comes.

Charlene, like many women in this phase of life, needs enjoyment in addition to rest. They need to reconnect with themselves as they take regular breaks. So that they can bounce back for their families in this fight day in and day out. Charlene isn't sure, but she knows something has got to give so she can find herself again and enjoy the things of life. All of these ladies are longing for enjoyment and feeling rejuvenated. They don't know what it takes to get there, but each one is seeking help to find the answers.

Joy does not simply happen to us, we have to choose joy!

And then keep choosing joy every day. In the terrific and in turmoil; in sickness and health. Make a choice now to choose moments of joy because life circumstances can very quickly change and are just as likely to sneak up on us over time.

These women are experiencing some of the most demanding challenges in these life experiences. The inability to find enjoyment and be fully themselves has left them discouraged and often feeling lifeless. There is a way to regain refreshment and rejuvenation. They want to keep at the work they are doing, whether it be their careers, their children, their ministry, their physical being, or even their family relationships.

We are here to walk alongside you... **Rejuvenation is achievable** in all these circumstances.

There is hope.

I'm Over 40 and I Know Some Stuff Now!

Chats with Specialists in their Fields.

Cristina Aguilera

An Imposter looking for My Ducks!

Engineer, Disciple, & Academic

Note: *The "impostor phenomenon" (aka "imposter syndrome") was first described by American clinical psychologists Pauline Clance and Suzanne Imes in 1978 as an "internal experience of intellectual phoniness" experienced by those with "outstanding academic and professional achievements." Since Grandma Eve, this has been a pretty standard game of mental hockey that women play! My mama understood this because long before Clance and Imes used the term Imposter Syndrome, my mama used the phrase, "Fake it till you make it!" and God will give you the courage to face it!" The idea is that it is His strength and ability, not ours. Cristina lives a life ready to jump into the next adventure Abba brings her; not because she can, but because He can! Cristina is one of the most courageous women I know!*

~ TLC

I have come to accept and embrace the fact that I am not enough and that I will never be enough. God did not make me to be everything for everyone around me, that is God's place. I can try to be a good daughter, friend, neighbor, sister, employee, coworker, etc., but I cannot be everything that my mom, friends, brother, and others need or want, God did not give me shoulders to carry that burden because it is not for me to carry. Realizing and accepting that God created me with limits has been freeing for me. I have limited time, health abilities, energy, financial resources, etc.

This world puts so much pressure on us every single day, if we try to run the race according to what everyone expects, and even ourselves, we will be permanently exhausted pigeons.

- Anonymous. Design by Holly Richardson.

Weakness is the place to find strength... It's one of the Biblical paradoxes, but it's true!

" But he said to me, 'My grace is sufficient for you, for my power is made perfect in weakness. Therefore, I will boast all the more gladly about my weaknesses, so that Christ's power may rest on me."

~ 2 Corinthians 12:9

For years, I did not like this passage. The independent woman in me resisted the idea of acknowledging my weakness...what do you mean I cannot do just about anything I put my mind to, by myself, without help?

It wasn't until I ended up in the ER dangerously close to a diabetic coma (unable to breathe well, extremely dehydrated, with blurred vision, etc.) that I started to accept that I truly am weak and that I cannot do things on my own. God created me to be dependent on Him and others. That night and in the coming weeks, He used his children to take care of me and bless me beyond my expectations. My sisters, the ones that God has given me here in Fort Worth, helped me when I did not even have the strength to take showers. I am still learning, because you know…I am a long-life learner, and I forget easily, and I default to the old ways. But His grace is enough.

As per the impostor syndrome, I too suffer from it, I always have. Every time I start a new position I would look around and wonder when people would find out that I really did not know "all that there was to know about the job." I still tell God, from time to time, that I am sure He could have found a better candidate to do "this" than me. But then I am reminded that He is God, and I am not, He is infinitely wise, and I am not. He is the master weaver of my life, only He has the vantage point to see the finished product and how every opportunity and job will fit together. If He has decided to open a door and allowed me to be positioned in a place that is unknown and feels uncomfortable, He will provide what I need to do what He asks of me…even when I don't feel that I have all my ducks in a row, especially when I don't.

Kate Jordan

Add a Dash of Authenticity!
Mom, Leader, & Friend

"The core of authenticity is the courage to be imperfect, vulnerable, and to set boundaries." - Brené Brown, Huffington Foundation

As Christians, we are called to live our faith authentically. This begins with knowing who we are in our flesh, and knowing who we are in Christ. And then, actually **believing,** *who we are in Christ. When we understand the truth of our own humanity and wretchedness, we can lay it all out on the table, because stepping into our identity in Christ allows us to own the value He places on our soul, permanently... 2 Corinthians 12:9 is pretty clear that His grace is sufficient, it's also unmerited, alongside his favor and blessing. Could you imagine if we made a daily practice to look at ourselves in the mirror, speak the power of scripture over our lives and attempt to take our self-talk, and ungodly emotional ties captive... and tell ourselves to choose to live authentically in His sufficiency? Wow... that sounds relieving!*

~ TLC

My 20s were an interesting time for me. I married young, literally on the day I graduated from college at twenty-one years old. Shortly after my first anniversary, I learned I was expecting my first child, the second one came just fourteen months later, and the third one soon after. Three children within four years, and I was twenty-seven. I found myself in a 'Mothers of Preschoolers' (MOPS) group and after attending my first meeting I was placed in leadership. Two years later, I was running a chapter, leading a steering committee of ten wonderful women. I had a husband on active duty in the military, so he was often away. We were always stationed on one coast or the other and all our family was in the middle, hundreds of miles away in Texas and Oklahoma. Let's just say, I was going it alone as a mom much of the time, and sometimes things got rocky!

I was talking to one of my friends from MOPS about the 7:00 pm witching hour at my house, the time after dinner when I was trying to get three kids successfully bathed and ready for bed. The time when the wheels always seemed to fall off. One, two, or sometimes all three kids started crying. Somebody wanted something when I was trying to help someone else. There was water all over the bathroom floor, a child who that morning was perfectly capable of getting dressed was suddenly unable to don her pajamas, and nobody in my little band of babes was the least bit interested in going to bed, despite being over-tired and cranky. I was venting about the fiasco I'd somehow survived the night before to a good friend and co-leader in my MOPS group. As my friend listened, her eyes grew wider and wider. "You mean that happens to YOU?" she breathed.

I was a little taken aback. I thought, "What do you mean? It's a three-ring circus at my house! It's three preschoolers and just one me. My family is literally a thousand miles away and my husband has been out in the desert for two weeks doing field exercises. We are hanging on by our toenails." I'm pretty sure something to that effect came out of my mouth. After all, this was one of my closest friends.

She replied with something along the lines of this. "I just thought you always had everything together. That your three little ones would smile sweetly as you tucked them in bed in your clean and beautifully appointed house."

And that's when I realized. I was busy trying to be a leader, to be an example, mostly for women who were older than me because my family came early. But in doing that, I left out a key ingredient. AUTHENTICITY. I wasn't intentionally trying to fool anyone into thinking I had it all together, but somehow that's what I portrayed. They didn't see me scrambling around like a madwoman trying to get the house clean before they came over. They didn't know I was riding the same struggle bus they were. It intimidated my peers. Even some of my close friends were a little afraid of me because they thought they would never measure up to someone who they perceived as a paragon. (Which was ridiculous!)

So, I changed my tactics. I started sharing not just the victories but my struggles, with the MOPS women and with everyone else. The hard stuff. The REAL stuff. I started when my kids were young. Admitting the fact that there were already Cheerios scattered across the floor again before I even had the cord wound up on the vacuum cleaner, and sometimes I thought if I had to listen to Barney sing one more song, I was going to lose my mind. Even though I adored my children, sometimes I just needed to talk to an adult or have a plate of food without a little person sharing it with me.

And you know what happened? People started being real with me too. They felt able to be more themselves. Have I completely arrived at this topic? No, and I probably won't this side of glory. I'll admit if I'm not careful, I still intimidate people sometimes.

I'm... a lot.

A big personality, and if there is a leadership vacuum, I will fill it. That's just me. But now that I'm in my 50's I know that it's the challenges, the grit, that not only mold us into our Father's image but strengthen us and make us interesting. And that's what makes us relatable. The realities I share with others now that I'm an empty nester are different, but they are just as real.

I guess when you distill it down, what I know is this: I am far more relatable, believable, and approachable when I let people see who I really am. It is moments of clarity like these that the Lord can use to wake us up and point us in a new direction. And for me, that's when He started to use the realities of my story to encourage others.

Well Done Good & Faithful

Spotlights on Organizations & Groups "Doing it well!"

Laughter and joy are gifts from God, and as Christians, we should embrace and cultivate them in our lives. God created a world filled with wonders and delights that can bring a smile to our faces and laughter to our hearts. It's important to understand the responsibility and importance of approaching comedy with discernment, ensuring that the humor we engage with aligns with God's values of love, purity, and kindness.

"Comedy is tragedy plus time."
~ *Carol Burnett*

Truth! Preach it, Carol! You're probably starting to see a theme in the plethora of stories from our lives… I'm convinced that God gives us 'ill-timed' moments of comedic relief amid precarious situations, which are like pressure relief valves for life!

By incorporating rejuvenation and using humor responsibly, we can intentionally uplift and edify others.

Christians, as members of the worldwide Church, have a unique opportunity to bring a sense of peace and satisfaction through joy and laughter into the lives of those around us. Let us remember that laughter is a reflection of the joy we find in God's presence and a testament to the goodness and humor He has instilled in His creation.

Me, Myself, & I'm His

~ Christy Parker

Chief Humorous Officer
<u>*Website:*</u> *Nope! Not gonna happen!*

> <u>Mission:</u> Officially I teach and train companies in the eastern hemisphere of the world in leadership and cultural intelligence. Technically, I know I was created to bring God glory, but I'm better at screwing things up in my humanity, so I'm pretty sure I exist for His personal viewing pleasure… I have a feeling He is watching my daily crazy life simply for His own comedic enjoyment!

Ok, so "Christy Parker" is not this sister's real name, but she is a dear friend that has been taking the Word of God throughout Southeast Asia and beyond with comedy and heartfelt stories of His power and intervention in and among closed nations. Due to the people and places, she encounters, her identity and company names are being withheld. I asked 'Christy' if she would be a part of this project and answer a few interview questions, to which she replied, "Why? I'm the worst!" After we giggled for a minute, I told her, "THAT!" That's exactly why! Christy and I met in Great Britain in 2002 and worked together in Phuket, Thailand on a Tsunami-Relief project in 2005. We needed each other's humor and compassion just to be of use during that devastating situation. We have remained close friends since, and I hope you enjoy hearing part of her heart, humor, and ministry poured out on the page. So, grab a cup of coffee and read this through the lens of humor, knowing my sweet friend is full of life and quick-wit! I feel funnier when I'm with her!

~ TLC

Interview Content with *Christy Parker*

How many years have you been in your field? What led you to this field?

A long time! I'm tired just thinking about it... I might need to revisit the Rest Culture section of the book before continuing this interview.

I can say that officially I have been doing this since before the turn of the century!

I heard an announcer introduce a speaker like that a few weeks ago, so I was expecting to see someone a bit mature, you know, who could have played basketball with Methuselah? But he had the nerve to walk out and be my age! What?!! And then I started to think about it... that's me... I actually did start traveling, speaking, and training in the 90s... so booyah! That's my final answer! Since before the turn of the century!

Tell us about your training or schooling.

The school of life! At least that's where most of my material comes from! My undergrad is in pre-medicine, and I received my medical degree in Germany. In my second life, I began studying psychology and anthropology because let's face it, humans are hysterical and worth intensive study! I actually met Tonya in Great Britain while we were working together at Cambridge Literacy Conferences. Ton was my trainer in cultural intelligence and utilizing Trauma-informed lenses when engaging with people from difficult places in life. The way I see it, if you disagree with any of my training materials, we can blame it on Ton. Wait, am I able to call you Ton in this interview, or is legitimately professional? (You can call me Ton, that's perfectly fine. As I laugh and shake my head, she keeps going without skipping a beat!)

I was a professional sandwich artist, thank you Subway for sparking the creative side of my culinary skills, though that's where they also end.

Additionally, I was trained in the art of Mary Kay consulting - it was a short-lived career, but my eye-makeup game really went up at the turn of the century! See what I did there?! Used the century phrase again, yes!

I still know how to make myself look fabulous, I'm just too tired now to bother. I'd rather wear a hijab, that's probably the real reason why I continue living and working throughout Asia and the Middle East.

Tell us about your faith.

My faith is the entire reason for continuing to participate in this crazy turning planet! God has so graciously given me life. He saved me from myself. He gave me hope, a truly fabulous life plan, and an amazing family. He made my life more abundant than I could have ever imagined. And then He dared to give me perspective, favor, opportunity, and the ability to present leadership, cultural support, and the hope of the gospel through the lens of humor! I get to meet strangers, turn them into friends, and for those who are interested in hearing it, make them disciples.

Family?

My Church family has legitimately stepped up! I never knew my father, but my mother was amazing! She had a hard life in Singapore and died young, but my uncle stepped in and paid for schooling that allowed for an amazing pathway! It was in school at a student ministry meeting that I discovered God was real! My mind was blown, and my life has never been the same! With the help of my 'Code Grape' tribe, I have never been without family!

Tell us about your organization.

I do have an international executive training company, but my heart for making disciples doesn't get published in our materials. What I do get to do, is share the truth! I get to use the funny commentaries of life and the brilliant answers of hope that come from the gospel to help people grow in their professional skills. Tonya and I have been involved in educational training and disciple-making together since 2002, right after the turn of the century (point!). See, she's old now too! Younger than me, but you know, we're all just counting down the days till Heaven! Some of us are just closer than others!

I regularly incorporate John Maxwell material combined with everything else we present because it's recognized around the world, it doesn't seem to "offend" many governments, and yet it is full of Biblical wisdom! It's like a backdoor sneak attack of the Gospel of Hope!

When it comes to wellness, how has your organization stewarded the concept of Rest, Rejuvenation, Revive or Relaunch?

Well... ha! I said 'Well,' no pun intended. Right to the point, our team works hard on their professional craft. We are always learning and asking growth questions to add value to the tools we provide to our clients. We work hard to track and keep up high-quality training for business executives. We try to make personal wellness an important priority for individuals, and we have made joy and laughter a priority for our company, encouraging everyone to find new creative ways to enjoy and laugh through the course of their training and events. To answer the question at hand... *(she clears her throat, ha-humm)*

We offer cross-cultural methodology training that can help Fortune Global 500 companies (in Asia, Eastern Europe, and the Middle East) assess their own core competencies and then identify the areas in their core that need to recalibrate, so they can better perform and add value to their people, the business areas of their expertise, and of course to the world!

Did that sound inspiring? Were you inspired? I wish your readers could have heard the passion and enthusiasm in my voice, it was fantastic! I was in the zone, wasn't I, sis?... I even got a bit inspired myself and I give that elevator pitch all the time! I think I might actually be pretty decent at my job!

At this point, we were both laughing so hard on the WhatsApp video chat, I knew she had limited time, so I just went to the next question...

Tell us about your hobbies and passions.

I collect people. Oh, don't worry, not in a human trafficking kind of way, I'm very much opposed to that! I'm more of a networker and people come willingly... usually.

I just love how weird and wonderful they are. Tata always says, "Humans are the worst and they're the best... all at the same time!" I agree, and I'm pretty sure she stole that from scripture, so I think it's public material I can officially reuse!

Tell us how you apply one of the 4Rs in your daily life.

Since you started the interview by asking me about rejuvenation, I'll talk about that. I think for me, I tend to be drawn to anything cultural and anything with water. I find great joy in going out and trying new restaurants, God knows that I can't cook, so I count good restaurants as pure joy! And just for your readers, I don't want you to think I was using God's name in vain, that was a true statement. He is very aware of my inept ability in the kitchen. I know that many, many prayers have gone up to Him regarding my cooking, I'm sure several grunts have also been made that the Holy Spirit probably had to translate.

I get transformed from the worries of the world when I attend concerts, plays, musicals, dances, etc. Again, it's probably none of those things that I am absolutely amazed at because I have not a musical cell in my bloodstream.

I love to laugh, so I try to keep funny friends in my life. If we were friends, but we're not now for some reason, don't take it personally, I'm just saying, up your funny game a bit and let's revisit! I hope your readers will hear my humor come through my words. I'm imagining you getting a ton of "concern" mail from readers who are under the impression I'm a narcissist and concerned for my soul. Although there may be a hint of truth in that, I should probably end this interview and go pray about that right now.

Humor is probably more my hobby, but I do have a few specific comedians I really love to watch. Physical comedy has always had a soft spot in my heart, so of course, Lucille Ball was a model of mine. She was a physical comedy genius! I also found Studio C a few years ago and I'm a total addict. Most people get hooked on Netflix specials, I'm the kind of person who gets hooked on "Shoulder Angel" skits.

Any last words?

In all seriousness, life is too short to be too serious about things that don't make an eternal impact. Make relationships with other people a priority and make regular laughter a discipline! If you're having a difficult time smiling, start with finding another person who will stand still long enough to let you hug them for 10 - 15 seconds. I know it sounds like an unusual approach, but it works. You cannot hug another person for over 15 seconds and not produce a smile. And go make someone else smile or laugh - it's selfish because it always makes the giver feel good too!

UNFAULTED

Angela Lippens & Carin Baird

Mission: Unfaulted exists to build a foundation for young women who have aged out of the foster care system by helping them grow through community, sharing the gospel and providing education, to equip them to be successful, independent adults.

It has been such a beautiful sight to witness the sincere and in-secret work of both Angela and Carin through Unfaulted. Even as a newer organization, the impact has been so evident and continues to spread awareness in the communities they serve. Recently, we had the sweet honor of sharing in the joy of one of their ladies, whom I call a dear mentee. This young lady married a Godly man last year and is now expecting her first child to be born. Seeing testimonies like this has been a beautiful testimony and reflection of the redemptive power of Jesus Christ. Angela and Carin, thank you for your obedience and response to the burden the Lord placed on your hearts. Your impact is much larger than you may ever realize on this side of heaven.

~ Amy

Note: This interview was with both co-founders - Unfaulted was incorporated in 2019 by Angela Lippens, CEO, and co-founder Carin Bird, COO.

Interview Content with
Angela & Carin

Tell us a little bit about you, your background, and your time with the ministry.

Angela: In 2016, I found myself in a place of deep reflection, sensing that something essential was missing from my life. I turned to God in prayer, earnestly seeking to align my heart with His and to understand His purpose for me. It was during this prayerful journey that the Holy Spirit illuminated a pressing concern: young individuals were aging out of foster care, and distressingly little was being done to support them. This revelation led me to delve into the world of foster care, particularly the challenges faced by those who transitioned out of the system. The more I uncovered, the more my heart ached for the vulnerable youth in my community who, upon reaching the age of 18, found themselves without the crucial support they needed. I began by sharing this burden with a few close friends, asking them to join me in prayer as I discerned what God was calling me to do. At that moment, I felt ill-equipped and almost certain that God had chosen the wrong person for this mission. However, a dear friend and colleague, Carin Bird, took my request to heart. She persistently encouraged me and repeatedly asked what actions I was taking in response to God's calling. Although I appreciated her prayers, fear often held me back from taking concrete steps. During this time, I served as a children's pastor at Fellowship of the Parks in Haslet.

In September 2019, during the "IF: LEAD" conference in Dallas, a significant turning point occurred. It became evident to me that my friend and co-worker, Carin, was meant to be a partner in this journey. Although I hesitated to ask her, I was astounded when she immediately embraced the opportunity. Usually, I'm the fast-paced friend while Carin approaches decisions prayerfully and thoughtfully. Little did I know the profound transformation that had been taking place in her life, leading up to this pivotal moment.

Carin: In 2018, after sharing my thoughts with my husband about what Angela was doing with Unfaulted, he straightforwardly told me that she would ask me to be a part of it. I dismissed his comment, thinking it was presumptuous, especially because we were coworkers and friends. However, my husband remained resolute in his statement, simply saying, "Okay." Fast forward to 2019, when Angela and I were at a conference. During a break, Angela hesitantly asked if I would like to join her in partnering with Unfaulted. At that moment, I understood precisely what God was calling me to do, and without hesitation, I said yes.

Angela: In 2005, I graduated from East Texas Baptist University with a Bachelor of Science degree in Education. While my academic background and teaching career may not have had a direct connection to non-profit social work, I've come to realize how God has intricately woven these experiences into my journey. My deep understanding of childhood development, nurtured through my education, has enriched my work in the non-profit sector. I've also found immense joy in applying my love for learning by crafting and developing a curriculum for Unfaulted.

Carin: As an 18-year-old senior in high school, I decided to leave school and earn my GED ahead of schedule so that I could marry my high school sweetheart before he was deployed to Iraq. At 19, I embarked on what has become the most significant role in my life - being a mother. While I didn't pursue a college degree, I've discovered that dedication, perseverance, and unwavering determination can propel me toward success.

Angela: Throughout our 20-year marriage, my husband and I have been blessed with two wonderful boys, aged 12 and 14. But our family is far more expensive than just the four of us; our home has welcomed numerous individuals who, though not all related by blood, have become cherished members of our family. God's plan for us has always transcended the boundaries of a typical family structure.

Carin: My husband and I have been married for 18 years and have three amazing kids, who are 17, 15, and 9 years old. One of the biggest blessings has been watching my family step into this ministry work. It's not just myself or myself and my husband serving the young women in Unfaulted. Our whole family is committed to the relationships we have formed throughout this journey; all five of us have opened our hearts and our homes to welcome several young women.

Unfaulted is dedicated to empowering young women who have aged out of foster care by equipping them to thrive through the Gospel, community support, and education. Our unwavering mission is to embody the compassionate service of Christ in all that we do. From 2019 to the present day, Unfaulted has operated a vibrant program primarily run by dedicated volunteers. All proceeds have been directed toward providing direct services to over 50 young women who have aged out of foster care in the DFW metroplex. We've developed a comprehensive curriculum, classes, training sessions, and resource networks tailored to the unique needs of this vulnerable population.

Our mission is to enhance the prospects of young people transitioning from foster care, and we address these challenges through our strategic program. In our commitment to supporting young women who have aged out of foster care in DFW and the surrounding areas, our program is anchored by three foundational pillars: Community, The Gospel, and Education. These pillars have been meticulously designed to create a holistic program tailored to the specific needs of these resilient individuals.

Ministry is undeniably challenging. The work we do is a continuous, day-to-day commitment, as the needs of the young women we serve persist without pause. Nevertheless, as an organization, we firmly believe in mirroring God's example of rest. We make a deliberate effort to schedule days of rest every week. While flexibility may be required to accommodate the girls' needs, we never forgo that sacred day of rest, acknowledging its significance in our mission.

What do you do for fun? How do you incorporate Extraordinary Wellness into your life?

Angela: I have a deep passion for creativity, nature, spending quality time with loved ones, and immersing myself in the world of books. Stillness isn't my strong suit, so I've learned to find ways to honor the Lord in moments of rest. For me, this often involves sipping on a warm cup of tea while I sit on my back porch, engrossed in reading my Bible. My true sense of rejuvenation comes from the act of creation, whether it's breathing life into a new project, tending to my garden and witnessing the miracle of growth, or allowing my mind to roam freely in the realm of creativity.

Carin: I absolutely love spending quality time with my family; it's my way of cherishing those close bonds. Gardening and tending to plants while watching them flourish brings me immense joy. When it comes to decorating, I find it so rewarding to create cozy and inviting spaces. Thrifting is another fun hobby, as I enjoy the thrill of finding unique treasures. To ensure I incorporate rest into my busy life, I often take quiet moments to reflect, pray, and journal providing me with a sense of peace and rejuvenation.

What area of wellness do you need more of?

We aim to bring a deliberate focus to the concept of re-launching. While it's typically driven by necessity, we aspire to infuse intention into this phase by prioritizing rest, rejuvenation, and revival before embarking on the journey of re-launch.

Bless Your Heart

Faux Pas' and embarrassing or tactless acts or remarks in the crazy social situations we find ourselves!

When I read the title, "My Mother's Aunt Twice Removed," it first sounded like an interesting Siamese-twin separation story! But as we chatted, it sounded all too familiar! As Shari and I were first talking about the "well-meaning" comments people make when they're not sure how to respond, the stories just flooded from both of our minds. Anyone who has ever had the opportunity to walk through a serious, life-threatening, or debilitating disease will identify! Again, it's a great opportunity to laugh and extend grace... but if you've never experienced it or felt the 'squirm', you might be the one making the "bless your heart" statement. It's just food for thought! And...Here's hoping these short stories allow you to either identify or giggle a little at our humanity!

~ TLC

// My Mother's Aunt Twice Removed //

|| By Shari Walker ||

When telling someone of my diagnosis for the first time, it never fails: they have a distant relative who had the same thing! It's often an aunt… almost always an aunt! You can see it on their face. They look off in the distance and search their memory bank to make some kind of connection to communicate so they can identify and communicate that they understand what I am going through. Meanwhile, I'm watching the face and wondering if they are having a stroke.

This sentiment is smothered in good intentions. But it is simply an attempt at empathy that falls just short.

// My Aunt's Cat had Cancer Too, but She's Dead Now //

|| By Tonya Lincoln ||

So many questions, right? Is it the aunt or the cat that died? Don't worry, it was the cat, all is right with the world!

Shaletha, a good friend and school administrator I worked with for over 15 years, had asked if I could come to share my story and conduct training with her new principals in the district. So, after a great day of training, I finally got to meet a few of them in person. She was so excited to introduce me to a few of the new young principals she had been mentoring. So, Letha brings me over and shares with one young lady, "Tonya's the professor that I was telling you about who survived multiple cancers and a couple of transplants." To which this young new principal says, "Oh wow, that's amazing, my aunt's cat had two kinds of cancer, and she survived her cancer too." To which, I responded as best as I could with, "Oh, I'm sorry to hear that"... "but, I am glad she's doing well now." To which she responded, "Oh, no, she's dead now, but she did survive two cancers. And it's ok because my aunt now has a new cat." With a little shock and as much composure as I could, I simply said, "Thank you for sharing" and congratulated their family for walking through that traumatic experience. I turned to look at my sweet friend, who was simply stunned, standing with a look of bewilderment, mouth dropped open, and all she could do for the next hour was say, "I'm so sorry... I'm not even sure what that was!" And we still laugh at that situation to this day!

// Mom Mishaps //

|| By Emily Bryant ||

"Awe, Rejuvenate with COVID!"
It sounds like a Calgon commercial gone bad!

When you think of COVID, I'm sure you're thinking it's quite the opposite of rejuvenation. I did… until I didn't!

Having a child starting middle school, two littles in elementary, and a potty-training toddler, I felt ill-equipped to meet their wide variety of educational, nutritional, and entertainment needs. James, my husband, was considered an essential worker since he fell under the construction umbrella. With him working every day, it was on me to make sure these kids were taken care of. My personal goal was to keep these small humans alive and somewhat educated! With three laptops and a naked toddler, we began our journey into online school in the fall of 2020.

It was not beyond me that EVERYONE was out of their element. I was a parent, my kids were students, and the teachers were forced into teaching online- many for the first time. I will never forget our first day. I got the 3 school-aged kids in separate areas of the house with 3 separate computers and schedules. All I had to do was get them online, and we would be moving in the right direction. I WAS NOT GETTING THEM ALL ONLINE. One job! Get it together!

I would get the first child signed in under the new district portal, but when I tried to sign in for the second child, the portal would only recognize the first child and wouldn't let me switch. A few hours later, I proudly got them all online using three different browsers. Wyatt was Safari, Avery was Firefox, and Lucy was Google Chrome. SERIOUSLY?! At least we had found a workaround!! Being in three different grades, there were very different expectations. My 1st grader was expected to sit and listen to her teacher for most of the day with a few breaks here and there. The 4th grader was expected to switch between three different teachers at specific times and to complete online assignments, and the new middle schooler was expected to login seven different times to seven different teachers with different sets of rules, expectations, assignments, and projects. I prayed often for God to help us and give us patience. I found myself bouncing from room to room asking things like, "Did you log in to reading?", "Why are you eating right now?", "It's 1:32. You should be logged into math by 1:25. You're missing the beginning of class! What are you doing?"

One day early on, I looked out the window and saw my 6th grader weed-eating the lawn in the middle of his class. When I threw my hands up and asked what he was doing, he replied, "I saw someone leave the Zoom meeting and I just thought it was over." Misfires such as this seemed to be occurring at a very alarming rate. My 1st grader was rolling around on the floor during her lesson, the 4th grader was making snacks while she was supposed to be in class, and the 6th grader was doing yard work. To top it off, we had interesting potty-training issues with the naked toddler! Sometimes it was messy and sometimes it wasn't, everyone with children understands that comment! Sometimes, the dog would help us locate the diapers and more, let's just say there were no kisses for the dog during that time period!!!! I often shook my head in disbelief that these things were happening and on a daily basis. For a time, every day became a day just to get through. Again, my personal mantra, "Just keep the small humans alive today!" When they got offline from school, they would immediately shift to video games and TV. It was a daily battle to cut screen time, and it was challenging for us all.

It took a while to establish a rhythm during this time, but eventually we did. The older two kids started doing online school with a couple of friends, and I was able to focus on keeping the younger two in check. Everyone got a timer with pre-set alarm times for the different classes, so the schedule checking was a little less like playing 'Whack-a-mole' now. We were adapting. Through these small changes and simply getting used to the way things were, James and I began to ask ourselves: "How can we use this society-induced 'pause' for something good? Can we go back to living more simply, find enjoyment in the small things, and regulate ourselves in this new rhythm?" The answer was slowly unfolding before us. The boredom we felt during many of the days caused us to seek out new hobbies and interests. My son began fishing in the river behind our neighborhood and occasionally at a nearby lake. He was able to safely socially distance himself and be with his buddies. My husband joined in when he could, and they both became avid fishermen. My daughter fostered friendships with neighbors and classmates that she had not previously entertained. She gained a beautiful friendship because of this time period. We visited with neighbors and strangers just to get out of the house. We went walking with friends to see them. My six-year-old learned to ride a bike. She was so proud of herself. She was becoming so independent. My youngest eventually learned how to use the toilet. HUGE WINS in the Bryant household.

It's rather remarkable when you step back and look at the totality of the situation... somehow God was able to weave something REJUVENATING into all our lives through something scary, inconvenient, difficult, and sometimes disgusting. That sounds just like our God, doesn't it?!

Oh, in case you're wondering, you'll be happy to know, I did it! My one job… I kept all four small humans alive, mostly sane, decently educated, and I think maybe even a bit more socially regulated than before we encountered COVID, go figure!

// It's True, I Heard it Once! //

|| By Ann Sullivan ||

Global Sticky Situations |
Brownie - The Mzungu Matatu & the Kenyan Bobsled Team

In 2008, a humanitarian crisis brought on by post-election violence erupted in Kenya, Africa. Tonya and I had the opportunity to witness the entire spectrum of events play out from the very beginning while we were living and serving in Nairobi and beyond. We were supposed to be going to Tanzania to help set up a Teacher's College, but the political climate in Kenya gave us pause to stay and minister there. And even though the State Department had recommended all Americans leave, we were asked by a few others if it would be possible for us to stay. So, with much prayer and petition before the Lord, we knew we were supposed to be there and serve those in Kenya during this tumultuous time.

While in Kenya, Tonya purchased a vehicle that was used to transport us all over Nairobi and the Rift Valley, the Masai Mara, and beyond! It was rather impressive for two white chicks to be driving the expanse of the country in a mostly working van... well, impressive or foolish is a fine line sometimes.

This van was multiple shades of brown, so many shades of brown, and was covered in dust for which the van inherited the moniker "Brownie." Awe, Brownie good times. Good memories! She had a lot of quirks, so many quirks, but we LOVED her anyway. One of her unique features was that she had faulty electrical wiring. It's not as bad as it sounds. In Kenya, the potholes, at that time, were SO prolific that most people would drive on the side of the road and on sidewalks, when available, to avoid them. When we did happen to hit a pothole, the lights on the dashboard would suddenly turn on and start to work, it was magical! You never knew exactly what was going to come on, or off for that matter. She also had a faulty gas gauge, that one wasn't as much fun. That made it incredibly difficult to know when her tank was empty, or even close. I forgot to mention that the only way to start Brownie from a dead start, was to "pop" the manual clutch... that became one of her endearing features, except when it wasn't.

Because of these "quirks", we found ourselves starting Brownie all over Kenya, including within the perimeter of Masai Mara National Reserve, where we saw wild animals (giraffes, hippos, elephants, lions, zebras, etc.) up close. We discovered that if diplomacy, teaching, speaking, or non-profit "executive'ing" ever got boring for Tonya, she always has a career as a driver in Kenya... She became a total pro at "popping the clutch" on a manual vehicle & driving on the right-hand side of the vehicle.

Kenya is well known for their matatu buses which have two important employees... the driver, and the conductor, or money collector! The driver's whole job is to keep everyone alive and when possible, out of accidents through all the dangerous traffic and crazy drivers in Nairobi! Not a small task, but neither is the conductor's job! The conductor's job is to collect the money while enticing customers through energy and entertainment. They are often swinging, acrobatic style, into and out of the van, sometimes they sing, but they're just all-around entertaining, at least the good ones are! And because Tonya was rather proficient at driving, I was delegated to the job of push-starting the vehicle and therefore I became our 'conductor.' I don't want to brag, but my swinging into and out of the van 'technique' got perfected over time... that's right, I'm now a professional bus acrobat!

When Tonya would finally get the popped clutch to start the car, I would have to run and use my new acrobatic skills to jump in the moving vehicle. Yes, you heard that right, I would push the van from behind with my 5ft 3in body almost parallel with the ground, see the van moving, gaining momentum, and I would run, catch up, and swing into the moving van! I still think we should have started charging admission tickets!

In Kenya, those with "white skin" are referred to as "Mzungu". Because jump-starting the van became a regular occurrence all over Kenya, we began to refer to ourselves as the "Mzungu Matatu" and better yet, we created our own "Mzungu Bobsled Team." I mean, it was just us, but we were in it, to win it! We often saw other "teams" practicing all over Kenya as well. More often than not, the Kenyan men would sit back and mesmerizingly watch in astonishment at this 5'3" Mzungu woman get the van going! If this helps, Tonya stands 6ft tall with shoes on, again, I'm 5'3, and that's with shoes on! We were an interesting site. We did learn how to be strategic though and 90% of the time, at least when it was available to us, Tonya would back up against a brick wall, building, or pole for push leverage!

Sometimes, I would have to contort my body and squeeze between the rear of the van and the cement wall to propel us forward to gain any momentum to jump-start the vehicle. It was definitely a sight to behold... and we, at the Mzungu Matatu Incorporated loved that our extra effort helped to provide much fodder for laughter... for Kenyan's and our fellow Mzungu's!

Unfortunately, as we attended our going away party in Kenya, we were informed that Brownie had been stolen. True story for another time! Hopefully, she provided them with as much joy and laughter as she did for us!

From your Mzungu Matatu Team, counting it ALL joy... We pray you too take the opportunity to view the world through Joy-colored lenses... it changes everything!

God's Got You
We'll Walk with You
You've Got This!

Practical Applications

Tools, devotions, journals, and prayers to help you tap into your privilege as a child of God, use your gorgeous guidebook, the Bible, step into your trusted Code Grape Tribe, and experience Extraordinary Wellness in your everyday!

|| By: Natalyia Rutherford ||

"Enter His gates with thanksgiving; go into His courts with praise. Give thanks to Him and bless His name."

~ Psalm 100:4

Rejuvenation is such a fun word! I can hardly say it without smiling or feeling some kind of excitement! To be honest, I think I could live my life stuck right here in this section. Not recommending that by any means, but I love to laugh and enjoy simple pleasures. However, even with that natural inclination, I KNOW it can be hard. The weight we carry - whether from clients in crisis, the pain our children experience, the traumas we encounter, or more -can be HEAVY. If the thought of finding joy seems overwhelming or impossible, you are not alone. This chapter is meant to inspire you to practice joy, whatever your circumstances. Try not to think of joy as a feeling. At GriefWorks, we tell our kids in groups that feelings change - they're fleeting. We want joy to be a practice or a mindset so that it can be attainable wherever you find yourself.

So, what does this look like for you? To help you brainstorm, I'm going to include Tonya's acrostic again because it has SO many great things to consider! Use it to fill out the table below. This one is focused just on you. Some sections may speak to you more than others so don't stress about filling out everything completely.

Rethinking Joy: List bible verses or inspirational quotes that will help you keep a mindset of joy

____

____

____

____

JUVENile: For those moments when we just have a minute or less, this is perfect because simplicity is key! Power naps, dance breaks, coloring, sensory walks... get creative!

____

____

____

____

Actions: Brainstorm activities to fill your day with joy, like taking a bath or getting a massage.

____
____
____
____

What songs pump you up and make you smile? Create a playlist of your top songs!

____
____
____
____

List your favorite exercises that give you that endorphin-high

____
____
____
____

Treasured Moments: How can you make memories and treasure the moments at hand? My favorites are often the simplest everyday things. Create an album (chatbooks!), start a video blog, or keep memories for your kids on a private social media page.

____
____
____
____

Intentional Celebrations: Celebrate the small things and the effort you've put in. I'm a big fan of adult achievement stickers, especially on harder days- it makes me smile and remember little wins still matter! And, of course, go BIG for the bigger wins! It may feel silly but doing this for ourselves cultivates healthy intrinsic value.

____
____
____
____

Omnipotent: Resting my mind by making powerful, but simple declarations of God's sovereignty and the prize of Him being in control. Keeping a prayer journal or gratitude journal is a great way to remind ourselves of this.

____
____
____
____

Nehemiah 8:10 Meditate on the Joy of the Lord. Meditation includes reading it, reflecting, remembering, recounting, sharing, and responding. What does it look like for you to fill your mind with this?

____
____
____
____

Here are some verses to get you started:

- *Nehemiah 8:10; Zeph. 3:17*
- *Isaiah 62:5; Jeremiah 32:41*
- *Deut. 30:9; Psalm 147:11*
- *Psalm 90:14; Psalm 16:11*

Awesome! Now you have a nice little self-care plan, hopefully with options that are for different time allowances.

Next, let's take this to your sphere of influence - because joy is extra sweet when shared! It will be the same setup as before but think through how you can practice this with those around you... family, friends, co-workers, church family, and community.

Remember, don't stress about filling every section! Focus on the ones that speak to you.

Rethinking Joy: List bible verses or inspirational quotes that will help you share a mindset of joy.

____

____

____

____

JUVENile: Play is transcendent across cultures, ages, and languages. Whether you have children, work with children, or just embrace your inner child - play is healing. Sometimes it's simple like throwing Christmas lights up for movie night, doing car karaoke, having a backward dinner (dessert first!), planning a progressive dinner, or hosting a Fancy Fondue night ... I'm noticing a trend; I think I'm hungry.

But you get the picture! Kim Sorgius at "Not Consumed" always has great ideas for simple fun - highly recommend.

____

____

____

____

Actions: I have very vivid memories of my mom and her friends having the silliest times together and with us! They TP'ed each other's houses, she often stopped to make my sisters and I do clown car drills (let's bring that back!), and my aunt would yell Merry Christmas at people while we did our newspaper route ... in June. What simple memories of fun do you have? What are some you could easily implement?

____

____

____

____

Treasured Moments: Really, all of these sections are great ways to practice joy AND create some great core memories. Some ideas for taking it a step further would be to send a thoughtful, handwritten thank you card - or, for those of you younger than millennials - tag a friend in a reel with some great memories. These are great ways to leave lasting treasured moments. What are some you can think of?

____

____

____

____

Intentional Celebrations: I love celebrations! Holidays, birthdays, wins - all of it. So many ways to have fun! One of my son's favorite ways to celebrate small accomplishments is "fart applause" (instead of clapping, give arm farts). Simple, silly, and oh-so fun! We've also had an "Extra Award" at work that we pass around. It's a trophy that has a drum major and it says, "You're so extra". Every time someone goes above and beyond at work, they get the trophy for a bit. The catch is, that person has to add something ridiculous to it. It has feathers, sequins, and is a hot fun mess! List some ideas that come to your mind for celebrating the best in those around you.

____

____

____

____

Omnipotent & Nehemiah 8:10 We've had some moments to plan for joy that comes through fun & silliness together but there's a seriousness to joy as well. It is essential in the manifestation of God's glory. If you remove the crown of joy from his people, His purpose to glorify Himself aborts. When we look at the state of the world, those without hope or those who have forgotten where their hope lies, it is up to you and me to show them. We must live this out, as we are called. Amid such global tragedy and pain, how do you show where your hope and joy lie?

____
____
____
____

"These things I have spoken to you, that my joy may be in you, and that your joy may be complete."

~ John 15:11

Jesus's promise to his disciples is that "my joy will be in you". So, Jesus must have joy himself that he is eager to share with them and us, not just a little joy, but complete or full joy.

Just as Jesus passed on his love and his peace to his disciples, so he also gave them his joy.

Later, in 2 Cor. 8:2 we see this joy grow by including others in it. This restless overflowing of joy emanates as love. "in a severe test of affliction, their abundance of joy and their extreme poverty have overflowed in a wealth of generosity."

Love is the restless abundance of joy in God that meets the needs of others.

REJUVENATION PRAYER

Father Lord,

Thank you for this joy that comes only from you.

This joy is our strength and our stronghold.

I confess Father that at times I forget you are in control. I forget the joy I have in you and instead get weighed down by the worries, the needs, and the pain of this world. You are their refuge, their Savior, not me.

Please help me practice my joy so that it overflows and glorifies You. May those around me come to see this restless joy and know it is rooted in You.

Amen.

Chapter Four

Revive Culture

REVIVE |
Rethinking a Biblical Approach to Revive

In this section, we are looking at all of the stories and information through the lens of **REVIVING** well. Extraordinary Wellness uses the following acronym to help us understand, plan for, and apply **REVIVAL** in our daily lives.

ReVIVE |

Scripture: Proverbs 18:15

"An intelligent heart acquires knowledge, and the ear of the wise seeks knowledge."

Proverbs 1:7

"The fear of the Lord is the beginning of knowledge; fools despise wisdom and instruction."

Definition: Begin equipped, seeking Wisdom, and choosing a Growth Mindset.

Revive is defined as having growth and being equipped with new tools through a rested and rejuvenated lens. Be revived through knowledge and seek wisdom from the Creator Himself. It is making time to learn new practices through new or 'revisited' content. It's being able to gain valuable tools after resetting, which can help you stay mentally sharp and improve your overall well-being.

Rethinking Revive | Restoring the joy of my salvation through Rest, Rejuvenation, and then through seeking Knowledge. It's gaining and practicing relevant, Life-Giving Tools. According to Philippians 4:9, these things bring His Knowledge & Peace to our lives.

Relevant Tools

- Personalized Assessments
- Professional Skill & Talent Acquisition
- Counsel Support - Mental health tools
- Pastoral Support - Spiritual health tools
- Medical Support - Physical health tools
- Peer Mentors - Mentoring & accountability tools
- Lifestyle Management - Life Skill Tools (time management, conflict resolution, healthy boundaries, life transitions, trauma care, intercultural intelligence, finances, business ownership, insurance, marriage, parenting, parent care, retirement, End of Life Care)

Victories Won & Sins Overcome | I am defined by my Identity in Christ.

- Recovery Model: Confession, Forgiveness, Repentance

- Paradigm Shift... from the world's mindset (church/ religion/ affiliations) to that of a Kingdom Citizen (for His Glory.)

Internal Tools | Tools that guide my thought processes include celebrating the disciplines of meditation, prayer, fasting, and study. CBT - Taking our thoughts captive!

*"Don't forget **self-talk**... Be aware of what I am saying to or about myself... failures or successes. Who does He say that I am?"*

Visible Tools | Tools that reveal and prepare us for what we need to improve the world around us: simplicity, solitude, submission, and service.

Engagement Tools | Community engagement and accountability through confession, worship, guidance, (Swift kick in the rear!), and celebration

Plus... Communication Development (Local language, relationship language, parental language, and confession language.)

Create a Culture of Revival

Remember, if culture is described as the characteristics of everyday existence (such as diversions or a way of life), usually shared by people in a common place or time, how can I be more intentional about living a revived life? Having a growth mindset or choosing to be a life-long learner is one of the greatest gifts we can give ourselves. To know that there is always more I can learn to become better, to think better, to behave better, to love better… to live better! When I realize I don't know everything, and I don't always have to be 'right,' I permit myself to grow.

Make Revival Culture a Practice

What does a Culture of Revival look like? What could it look like? Can you create a regular practice of gleaning and growing in His Word? Can you choose to have a growth mindset approach to gaining new and useful knowledge for yourself and others?

- Assume there is always a new nugget of knowledge God has for you when you encounter conversations and learning opportunities.

- Seek out courses and training in areas that you know will help you grow and benefit your sphere of influence.

- Choose to be a part of an in-depth Bible study, prayer team, and/or worship team… not as the leader, but as a participant who is asking the Father to reveal and teach you something new!

If You're Trying to Drive Me Crazy, It's Too Late!

Real Stories, Real Woman, Real Themes of Life
By: Aimee Rhodes

We are here to tell you **REVIVAL** is achievable in all the true stories you are about to read! **There is hope!**

Single, Professional Woman

Kendra, this entire time, has felt stuck, powerless, and resigned to her normal pattern of showering, getting dressed, driving to work, doing her job, returning home, eating, and going to bed. She wants to make changes and feels back on her feet and excited about her role in her community, but really knows it's all in her head. She knows some basic steps to help get her mind going but often gets stuck on certain issues and can't seem to just break from the bondage and create new patterns to help her rebound from her burnout phase. She has consumed so many self-help books and has gotten so many confusing messages on how to break the patterns that keep her in a perpetual state of compassion fatigue and burnout.

One book even suggested just getting passionate about something else and doing more things. While it was well intended, Kendra realizes that she needs to really get in her rest, and work on enjoying her hobbies she recently discovered. She isn't ready to take on a brand-new project just yet. She isn't sure if she even should.

She has big dreams to start a program to work with young women who have experienced generational trauma and help them end the cycles that led to those patterns. She realizes it would be far too much work for now but would like to at least enjoy her current job again and learn as much as she can from her managers and leaders. She knows their systems are really organized and wants to be mentored so she can understand the game. She knows her passion remains for this wild and crazy field. She feels she has a better handle on things but is still just not fully back to herself. She wants that spark, that fire from within. She just wants to leave the crispy edges out of the picture this time. "But how?" she thinks to herself. She's told it's possible but is doubting the ability for it to come back. It has been a while since she's been on this train and while she sees a light at the end of the tunnel, she isn't quite sure she can trust its daylight on the other side. It just might be another train coming in the opposite direction.

Living with Chronic Illness/Terminal Illnesses

Maya finally got to get out of the house and spend time on her porch holding court with her fellow girlies. She appears refreshed by their recent visit. She still wants to be able to break free from the never-ending cycle of medications, treatments, and steady but slow workouts. She thinks she can pull herself up by the bootstraps and just push through like all the women before her.

Maya has worked along with a few professionals who offered to teach her body movement exercises and truly be compassionate to herself in this season. Maya has tried the tools and thinks she can take them on little by little. Anything is better than nothing.

Maya cannot seem to get over the idea of having others come into her space and do her laundry for her or change out her bedding. She barely lets her husband help with the dishes. She doesn't want to appear weak to anyone. Weakness means she's vulnerable and that she just might not beat this thing.

Maya knows something has to change as she won't be able to work after her chemo treatment for at least two weeks. She knows she cannot do everything she once did. She tries to reason and rationalize with herself all the reasons it is good to let people help. Mentally, she knows it's okay to ask for help, but just can't seem to allow herself to receive it from anyone. She dreams of being able to hire extra help but knows that it is out of the budget and just goes against everything in the fiber of her being. "I'm driving myself crazy with this," she puffs out as she talks to herself while loading the laundry one more time before her back gives out.

Maya comes from a strong line of women in her family who had to often suck it up to keep up with the household. She feels like asking for help is just another form of complaining and not being grateful. Her friends are willing and waiting to chip in. Maya just has to be willing to receive the help they are offering.

Mamahood, from Littles to Hormonal Teenagers

Fatima has adjusted to her mother-in-law's presence in the home and is finally ready to return to work. Fatima can't help but feel guilty that she is leaving her children each day to be watched by her mother-in-law. She tells her husband over breakfast, "I just feel like your mom is raising our kids." Fatima has worked incredibly hard the last few years, changing her career by returning to school and taking a licensing exam. She had hoped to add financial gain to the family so things would not feel so tight. She knows her husband never complains and wants her to do what she was made to do, but Fatima feels pulled between the two worlds of her small children and this career path she is on. She never suspected she would have four children under the age of five when she would need to start her clinical rotations. Fatima continues to put off this part of her next steps for fear of failing herself and her children.

Fatima meets up with her friend again with the teenagers since she hasn't quite taken that next leap. She asks about her friend and her teens. Her friend shares that her kids have each taken a stint with detention, making life choices that have her knee-deep in legal matters. The friend is pretty sure God is out to drive her crazy. But feels like she is already crazy for having her kids so close together.

Fatima reflects and worries that will be her story too. She doesn't want to miss out on her kids' soccer games and cheerleader competitions. But truly she doesn't know how to make it all work in the 24 hours she is given each day. She remarks to her friend she feels pressed to decide whether she should work full time and use her parents as babysitters full time. She looks up to the sky and cries out to God "it's too much and I just feel like I'm losing it. I know I can make this change, but something has to change!". She feels much too trapped by herself as her kids are still Velcro kids. She knows getting back to work on her goals will help her to feel connected to other adults and it's important for her to have this success, however, she just can't get over the mental block that she is abandoning her kids. The real problem is within her mindset.

Living Life with Older Parents in Late Stages of Life

Charlene continues with her caretaking but has become frayed at the edges and knows she needs a break from the caretaking. She cannot take it anymore. She feels like she made the wrong decision to bring her parents into her home. She is up day after day, and her once semi-balanced life is now fully focused on her parents, to go on medical leave full-time to care for them. She regrets doing so because now her constant companions are the grief of being the primary caretaker, her mother's dementia, and a week-old soup in the fridge. Charlene's hired nurses continue to come and help. They have even urged her to take the day off when they are there.

Charlene in her gut knows they are right especially since she feels like one pull of the thread, and she will completely unravel. She has discussed at length with her husband what to do but he's been more distant as his own parents' health problems have crept in.

Charlene and her husband are like ships passing in the night, attending to their aging parents' needs. Her husband, however, still works full time, and Charlene is growing somewhat resentful that he leaves the house at all. She just feels dragged down by all the duties she performs day in and day out.

In her mind, she feels guilty about putting her parents in a home. She knows it would alleviate a huge chunk of the burden and that they would also have more engagement than at home. She also takes pride in caring for her parents' needs and that they can afford to have them in their home. On the flip side, she feels as if she is losing herself. She furrows her brow and places it in her hands. Crying out how to decide which one is best. Charlene pauses, sighs, and makes a resolution. She is ready to make the decision.

REVIVING is about growth, life, perspective, and being equipped!

This stage is not an easy one, but it becomes phenomenally more doable when we come from the previous two R's. For Christians, reviving brings a growing interest in prayer, consumption of His Words, and the ability to take on new knowledge. Just as prayer precedes revival, prayer also sustains revival. When God is present, He cannot be ignored. Hunger for intimacy with Him is heightened and finds expression through prayer and seeking wisdom. Being in His presence will become the delight of our lives.

We are here to encourage you… Keep cycling through, because **Revival is attainable** in all our circumstances.

There is hope.

- It's a beautiful thing to watch joy grow from a choice, into a deeper characteristic of our worship. Joy becomes pure and will develop into joy overflowing.

- In periods of reviving, the desire to be entertained and to 'feel good' is revealed for what it truly is–a cheap imitation of godly joy.

- God Himself will take center stage, and the Lord Jesus will reign as the sole object of our adoration.

- God's Word will be exalted and authoritative over human experiences.

- The need to be entertained lessens, the desire to enjoy life with gratitude increases, and a desire to learn and grow abounds.

I'm Over 40 and I Know Some Stuff Now!

<u>Chats with Specialists in their Fields.</u>

Rebekah Romo

<u>Authentically Not Me!</u>

Mom, Leader, & Friend

When I first met Rebekah at an after-church picnic, I knew right away I'd found a friend with similar life experiences and a heart for Kingdom work. She is a military spouse, a committed mom, a devoted friend, and a remarkable warrior of faith who has 'been there' and done it all. A self-confessed wild child in her early 20s, today she is a pied piper in a tutu with a band of merry littles in her wake, serving as Children's Pastor at The Gathering Church -Veridian. When she isn't working with kids on Sundays, after school, or teaching high school, she's working on her doctorate! Rebekah knows how to get stuff done, but she always has time for people. If you need prayer, she's your gal. She's never met a stranger, and, in my experience, she is at all times willing to drop everything and listen, a Code Grape friend for sure! She is a woman who is constantly on the go, go, go, but who knows the value of stopping! love what she has to say about that!

~ Kate

Part I - I'M DONE!

I'm at the bottom of my tank right now as I write this. I'm done, so done. Yes. I'm a Christian. Yes, I am a Pastor. Yes, I am human. Somedays, I struggle. Today is one of those days. I don't want to do anything.

I don't want to talk to anyone; I don't want to cook, clean, think, or even pray. I want to run. Run away, but I'm too emotionally, physically, and spiritually exhausted to get up from this chair and do it.

I want to poof away. Not forever, well, maybe forever. Can I just go to heaven now? I don't want to die or kill myself, but I also don't want to live. I don't want to do anything. I'm not even sure how I'm formulating this sentence. You are actively reading a miracle in the making.

I'm not sure where my oomph went. Where did I spend it? Was it overscheduling, overthinking, over-controlling, over-trying, over-sharing, over-caring? Was it too much? Can I really be overspent from doing good things?

Forget it. I don't even want to think about it. This recliner and fluffy blanket envelop me, but don't fill me. I just want to sleep. To stop. To just be. But I don't want to think about what I have to do to get there. The simple act of taking a shower sounds like climbing Mount Kilimanjaro.

This isn't the first or even the fiftieth time I've hit the bottom of the barrel. I've done all the "good" things to fill back up:

- Long hot Epsom salt baths with a great movie and glass of wine
- Loud dance classes
- Sitting on the porch in a rocking chair, chatting with my incredible husband
- Girls' night out with my sisters
- Processing my issues out loud with my bestie
- Curling up on the couch with a warm blanket, fireplace, cup of coffee and the two cutest doggies curled up beside me.
- Eating Chocolate
- Gratefulness Journaling

They work for a little while, most of the time. Not this time. They are "good," and they help, oh how they help, but here I am. Empty. Done. My saving grace is knowing that in just three days, I'm leaving.

Nestled on the side of a broken-down country road across from an old neighborhood graveyard sits the entry to my rest. No talking, no doing anything. No phones. No emails. No serving. No ministering. No talking. Silence and solitude are just what I need to find Rest, Rejuvenate, Revive, and Relaunch.

The absence of noise and people is one of the greatest gifts God has given me. Typically, I love noise and people. I'm a children's Pastor who believes kids should be heard, and I love to be with people. I'm that weirdo person who naturally pulls out the stories from complete strangers and can stand in a gas station for two hours talking to a group of Muslim men about Jesus. True story. Typically. Not today. I am thankful for a deadline and an opportunity to write right now because it's my excuse not to answer the phone, text, or door.

This crazy obsession to be alone in silence started just a few years ago. I was 39, had a great relationship with my handsome Navy pilot husband who adored me, a 12-year-old daughter who loved ballet, and a 9-year-old son who loved to climb trees. I was living the American dream. But I was not satisfied, so I went back to college to try and fill that space in me that felt not- good-enough.

My first semester at Hope International University introduced me to one of the most painful yet rewarding experiences of my life, kind of like childbirth. A vivid memory of pain, but then it is erased by joy. Brace yourself; I turned off my phone for two whole hours.

I wish I could say it was because I was so holy and had great self-control, but it wasn't. I really wanted an "A" so I could get a better GPA than my husband. I know. Competition in marriage isn't good, but obviously, I have issues. Anyhow, back to the story.

Professor Jan Johnson gave us this crazy assignment. My reaction was, "You want me to do what? Turn my phone off and not talk to anyone? For two hours!" My mind raced through the possible scenarios of how the world would fall apart if I couldn't be reached. After all, I'm the get-it-done, save-everyone, try-it-all, plate-spinning, over-achieving Wonder Woman, Barbie, Xena Warrior Princess. So, I thought. Turns out. I'm not. No one is. They are all made up.

God did not create us to be everyone's everything. That's His place. My place is to be at His feet like Mary. Not worrying about all the things like Martha. But I get caught up in the here and now. The pride of life. The rush of accolades and accomplishments. But beneath the exhaustion, my heart pants for the One I truly love. Beneath the beat of the daily grind of life, my heart faintly cries words written by Zach Neese:

I wanna sit at your feet
Drink from the cup in Your hands
Lay back against You and breathe
Feel Your heartbeat
This love is so deep
It's more than I can stand
I melt in Your peace
It's overwhelming

This is where I want to be, where I will be, in just three days. I will lie in a white hammock beneath two giant oak trees as they release their fall leaves, doing nothing but letting my soul sit at His feet–absolutely nothing else. I won't even have to talk. Literally, it is a silent retreat center. Montserrat Jesuit Retreat House was created by God just for me. I'm God's Boo. I really am, and so are you.

There on that hammock, in the silence, in the solitude, there is space to hear the soft, gentle voice of the One my soul yearns to be with. There, in the absence of the things, my soul pours out its tears of regret, fears, and doubt at the feet of my Jesus.

When I get away from the noise, the to-do list, and even serving, I open a space in my being to just be with Him. The One who fills my being with hope, rest, imagination, forgiveness, and grace. The One who heals me. Even now, He gives me hope.

Just the thought of my vacation with my Jesus motivates me to hold on, to carry on. In three days, I will rise again. I will say my goodbyes to my sweet family, take a deep breath, joyfully turn off my phone, enter the gates, and finally exhale. For four days, I will just be with Him.

We will sit on a wooden swing and watch the sunrise over the lake. I will marvel at the works of His hands, and He will wrap me in the warmth of the sun's rays as He whispers how much He loves me. We will sit alone at our little classic brown table in the corner of the quiet, simple dining space as I will taste every bite with slow intention and amazement at how it was created. Time will flow gently as I sip a cup of soothing tea, take a pen in my hand, and color. I will use my gel pens to fill in the geometric patterns on the page, and He will use His Word that is hidden in my heart to invigorate my imagination.

Someday, in God's perfect timing, I will be with Him forever. Nothing between us. But for now, I'll be gentle with myself and give myself the same kind words I've spoken over other sisters in our tribe who have battled these same feelings. I will laugh, eat something delicious and healthy, drink coconut water, and increase my vitamin D intake.

I will go to sleep early and not feel guilty. My husband is an amazing father and will support anything the kids might need. I do not have to feel guilty for taking care of his wife and their mother. I am ok with not being ok. I don't have to hide the scars or the journey, I am not alone. I am surrounded by a tribe of beautiful prayer warriors who minister to me and they never cast judgment. I am holding on. I hold on to hope by sharing my testimony with you dear reader.

My life is for His glory, His story.
https://montserratretreat.org/
https://wordtoworship.com/song/8126#Google_vignette

* * *

Part II – ONE WEEK LATER

I drove as fast as I could to the retreat house, hurriedly checked in, and quickly unpacked. I threw my coat on, grabbed my blanket, and rushed out the door to start my journey to solitude. The canopy of ancient trees with falling leaves enveloped my sight as I walked the half mile from the room to our hammock. I felt my shoulders soften as my stride slowed down. There, in the near distance, the white hammock anchored to two gloriously giant oaks gently swayed in the fall breeze. My heart leaped with anticipation. I had been waiting for this moment of sweet surrender for far too long.

I fluffed my red and blue blanket across the surface of our hammock and exhaled as I laid back into the memory of the last time we were here. I spent most of the of the first day spilling all my tea, and everyone else's to Him. I made so many plans and told Him what we needed to do next. This time, knowing He already knew all the needs, desires, fears, and frustrations of my life, I decided to be in the present. To be in His presence.

I spent the next several minutes paying close attention to my breath. It was cold as I inhaled deeply but it warmed as it entered the depths of my lungs. The exhales grew slower and longer each time as I sank into the blanket. Intentionally changing my focus to my body, I noticed the tingles in my toes, the fresh cool breeze on my skin, and the softness of my shirt against my shoulders. Slowly, my attention turned to hearing the sounds around me. Not listening, hearing. Not examining where or what the noise was but experiencing the pitch in the dog's howl, the crescendo of the plane flying past, and the trills of the bird's songs. With another full breath, I inhaled the surrender of knowing He loves me and melted into the warmth of His presence.

Here, alone in His presence, time changes. The morning sun kissed my face, and time slowed to the rhythm of my breath. My thoughts flowed to the rhythm of His voice as He impressed my soul to choose joy, choose happiness, choose laughter.

How do I do that? Was my mother right when she told me to "just get happy"? Is it really a choice? Then, out of the blue, the brilliant idea to keep a joy journal popped into my mind. We all know where that came from Him. Not gratefulness or thankfulness, but moments in my life that have made me smile or laugh. Moments like when my daughter made a green smoothie, poured it into a jalapeno jar, and gave it to my son. Moments like when my husband said, "Follow me" and did a goofy walk, expecting us to mimic him and we did.

God is so smart. Of course, this is what I need. He says it clearly in His Word, and He stands by His Word. "God is not a human being, that he should lie, or a mortal, that he should change his mind. Has he promised, and will he not do it? Has he spoken, and will he not fulfill it?" (Numbers 23:19)

We are to be transformed by the renewing of our mind (Romans 12:2). Life's tragedies can hardwire our thoughts to run to the negative, but when we deliberately think about the things that are true, honorable, just, pure, pleasing, commendable, excellent, or praiseworthy then we start realizing that those perfect gifts of moments in time are "from above, coming down from the Father of lights, with whom there is no variation or shadow due to change (Philippians 4:8, James 1:17).

Songwriters Becky and Geron Davis skillfully described the truth when they penned the lyrics to "In the Presence of Jehovah."

"In the Presence of Jehovah"
In the presence of Jehovah
God Almighty, Prince of Peace
Troubles vanish, hearts are mended
In the presence of The King

This path of being in His presence, my beloved, is the path of life spoken of by the psalmist. In this path is the presence of God, where there is "fullness of joy" and "pleasures forevermore" (Psalms 16:11).

Praise be to God!

He chose me so that I can choose Joy.

Natasha Dudley Busick

Guilt Be Gone!

Teacher, Friend, & Lover of Souls

I was giving a few educational lectures in Boston and had a 45-minute break between seminars. I ran over to the Harvard Square Tea shop in need of hot tea with honey and while ordering, I heard a familiar voice over my shoulder. "Tonya? What are you doing here?" to my surprise, it was one of my Aunt Pam's best friends and one of my favorite people, Tash! She was on a university tour with her daughter. What are the odds? Here's the crazy part, a little over a year later, I'm back in Boston, but at Boston College this time. I'm going up the escalator and to my complete shock, who do I see? Tasha! She was coming down the escalator on the other side! Seriously? Tash lives in San Diego, I live in Fort Worth, these are like Vegas odds! God simply knew it was time, and we needed to see each other again! Tash shares a deep heart for the nations. She loves and prays fiercely, like our lives depend on it, because she knows it does! Love you sweet sister... see you in Boston, Tash!

~ TLC

When I was in my 20s, my parents lived in Nairobi, Kenya. While there, I went to an orphanage. Instead of just loving the children, I was filled with guilt and shame when I observed their lack and what I had in my life. They were wearing bits of tires for shoes. They lived in shacks. I couldn't fathom why they had so little, and I had so much.

Why was I born in America? I wanted to keep what I had and didn't want to give it up.

I actually grew up somewhat poor by American standards and was constantly surrounded by some of the wealthiest in the world. For most of my life, I went to prestigious private schools on scholarship and the other students had so many fancy cars, monstrous homes, beautiful clothes, and all of the latest gadgets. So, for me, having nice things was a luxury. When I arrived in Kenya, I really wanted an Ethiopian cross. They were beautiful and represented Christ and beauty to me. I was going to a Christian college at the time. One cost $20 in Kenya, which is a lot of money there, but as a broke college student, it was also a lot of money to me. I was very excited to wear it. I had been dreaming of getting one even before coming to Kenya. When I went to the orphanage it hung like ugly guilt and shame around my neck. I felt horrible and greedy. I had picked out the one that I could afford at the Nairobi Market, and I was very excited to wear it. While at the orphanage, one of the children asked for it and I didn't want to give it up. I knew about the story of the widow and the mite. I knew I should give it up, but it was so special to me and had been a really big deal to get it. I didn't give it to the child who asked me, and I felt horrible. I couldn't shake the experience. It ruined my visit. I cannot describe in words the feelings of guilt and sadness that I felt. It was hard for me to wear the cross without feeling wretched and picturing the children's feet with tires tied to them and the shacks and mud with which they lived.

Over time, the feelings didn't go away. They worsened. I majored in Political Science with an emphasis on International Relations because I wanted to change the world. While I was interning for the US Vice President later that year in Washington, DC, the guilty feelings from my experience at the orphanage just would not leave. I knew I needed help, and the National Presbyterian Church was offering free counseling for college students across the street from my university campus. As God would have it, my counselor was a former missionary to China. After she listened to me, she explained that it just wasn't possible to help everyone in the world and I could spend my days feeling guilty. I had to understand my limitations. She gave me the analogy about feeding someone versus teaching someone to fish. I could only do what I was called to do. It actually did help me. At the end of the semester, I decided not to work for the US Government and USAID as I had originally planned. I had interviewed people who worked for the government in positions that I wanted, and they had discouraged me from that path. I realized that all of my life experiences would make me a better teacher. I had worked with children at the International School in Kenya and loved it. I thought maybe I could change the world one child at a time instead of through the US government. I could help instill in them a love for the world.

I left Washington, DC, even though I had a position at Campaign Headquarters for President George Bush. I had in my heart to just go home to San Diego, even though I really had nothing left for me there. My friends and family had all moved. I prayed and wanted to go to the School of Evangelism (my church's totally rad Bible school). I couldn't believe God would let me do something as exciting as that! My friend had a dream that we would go together before she was even a Christian. She moved back from North Carolina and went with me.

I did become a teacher. I have been able to inspire my students each year to do something to change the world. They have come up with beautiful and radical ideas. From creating all school art fairs to help local refugees to fair trade chocolate fairs to raise awareness about slavery in the world, to raising money to build a well in Kenya, the children have come up with unique ways each year to make a difference. One year, they decided to create a refugee camp experience for the school. Each year, we went to visit Medical Teams International. One of my students decided to become a doctor because of that.

I no longer feel guilty about my limitations. I try to do my part by inspiring my students and blessing one student in Uganda I sponsor through World Vision. I was fortunate enough to live as a dorm parent to international students and bring them to church each week. I can say "no" more than I have been in the past when I realize it is not my gift. I worked with former male prostitutes when I was living in Portland to try to do my part in putting a stop to sex trafficking. I realized that I didn't seem to connect at all with female prostitutes. I know better than to do something that I am not called or gifted to do, so I can stay within my calling, which is clearly working with children.

Guilt still does plague me from time to time, but I can resist it faster and walk in Romans 8:1 and know that condemnation does not come from God. Most of all, I have learned what it is to love.

If I were to go back to that orphanage today, I would truly and wholeheartedly love those children without any guilt.

Natalyia Rutherford

<u>From Bummers to Boundaries!</u>

Teacher, Friend, & Lover of Souls

I received a call one morning that one of our single moms at Hope Farm had died in her sleep the night before. Unfortunately, her son, one of our 9-year-old young leaders at Hope Farm, had found his mom that morning. He went to wake her, to take him to Hope Farm summer camp. Our entire staff jumped into action to see how we could best help this precious family, but we too were in mourning. The first person I called was my friend Natalyia. She and her team jumped into action and days later came to sit and talk with our entire team. We learned how to grieve and walk through the situation with this family. Their team provided counseling and support to our young leader and his entire family. Natalyia and I have had the honor of working together now on several important projects and the more I know her, the more I praise God for her. I'm not even quite sure how I lived without her for so long! Should you or someone you know need support to work through grief, I cannot say enough wonderful things, but I will do my best to convince you to call my friend Natalyia & her Griefworks team... they will change your life!

~ TLC

When it comes to our own health and well-being, it's harder to practice the advice we give.

I first noticed this in the last few years (the end of my 30s). I work for a non-profit called ChristianWorks for Children and one of the roles I have is coordinating our children's grief support group, GriefWorks. The families that come have all experienced the death of someone they love.

Now, often when I share what I do, people look at me like "Well that sounds like a bummer" but I feel grief education is such a life skill because we all know grief isn't reserved just for death. We can grieve several things over a lifetime: a move, the end of a friendship, a lost job, divorce, illness, the dreams we had for ourselves or our family - so many changes. These skills we're giving to these kids and their caregivers will follow them throughout their lives. Every change they grieve, big or small, gives them a chance to practice and solidify these skills again. One of those skills is permitting yourself.

I came from a great family; a loving, churchgoing, service-oriented, amazing family. My dad worked a crazy number of hours to support us and ensure my mom could stay home, raising my sisters and me as long as possible. I remember my mom always 'doing' for others and I'm so proud to have inherited that from her. (Service is my love language!) We were taught to be respectful and helpful and, I'm not sure why but I somehow took it too far. For as long as I can remember, I always looked to someone else to tell me what to do. I behaved according to the expectations placed on me by those around me. Maybe it's the oldest child thing, the need to please, and all of that. It wasn't till I was in college and my former youth minister gave me the book "Boundaries" by Dr. Henry Cloud and Dr. James Townsend that I realized this was a problem for me.

At GriefWorks, most of our families that come are in survival mode. Grief is so overwhelming and so exhausting that they are doing good to cover basic needs. Sometimes, there is a lot of guilt with this and so we have them practice permitting themselves to say "no" to the extras. We also teach the kids in our groups that every feeling serves a purpose. There are no "bad" feelings. Sure, they're not all pleasant, some are downright painful, but the only way to get past it is to permit yourself to FEEL it. Sit with it, make friends with it. When our families really get it, you can see that weight lifted.

"I can say 'no'?"

"I'm not alone with this guilt?"

"My feelings aren't bad? They're valid?"

How many of us need this kind of validation so that we can give ourselves permission to do what we must to keep healthy?

I got better with my boundaries as I got older in some ways. Maybe marriage does that to you? Or having kids? Something, like not even being able to go to the bathroom by yourself, will drive you to enforce some boundaries! But I was still struggling. I was burned out - not just in one area either. If it was all in one area that might have made it easier, but it wasn't. It was all in areas that I felt God called me to marriage, motherhood, my work, and my church. None of these were unimportant things! Still, I had lost my motivation and my joy in a lot of it, especially the last two. I think I was reaching a critical point and God was talking to me through every avenue - the search committee group I was on at church, my Rooted bible study group, and especially GriefWorks. I had to start saying "no". I had to sit with this apathy and figure out how to work through it. And I did. With the help of my husband, we identified ways to step back from serving at church so we could prioritize time with God individually and as a family. I hope my kids recognize this step and understand you can't pour from an empty cup. Service for God cannot replace intimacy with God. I gave myself permission to say "no" to things I *thought* God was calling me to and replaced it with rest in Him, and intimacy with Him.

Every day I'm inspired by the families at GriefWorks and I'm thankful for their example of doing the hard work. Just like with our support groups, it's always easier when you have another person to validate your feelings. My husband was a blessing in helping me give myself that permission. My supervisor also listened, and we devised a plan so that I could keep giving my best with energy and passion. Find those people in your life to encourage you and keep you accountable.

Well Done Good & Faithful

Spotlights on Organizations & Groups "Doing it well!"

Reviving is all about equipping the Church. Equipping others to serve shows church members we want grace to build the ministry, not our ambitiousness, savvy leadership, delegation skills, or, even worse, our self-sufficiency. Equipping unifies the church around Jesus, not us.

"God is a specialist at making something useful and beautiful out of something broken and confused."

~ Charles R. Swindoll

Shalom Foundation

~ Caylen Santos

Chief Executive Officer
www.theshalomfoundation.org

Mission: We exist to bring healing and hope to underprivileged children in Guatemala by providing free, life-changing medical and nutritional care to those who need it most.

I'm still amazed and so proud when I learned about the work Caylen and the Shalom Foundation are doing. I watched a precious, beautiful little girl in pigtails learn how to ride her bike at the OBU campus and grow into a stunning woman of God! From visiting and working alongside her family in Asia and throughout the Middle East, I have seen this TCK (third culture kid) find her unique, strategic, & very important place in Kingdom building! I'm forever indebted to your family for their love and guidance… and I'm forever a HUGE Caylen fan! Keep reviving well and keep up the life-changing work!

~ TLC

Interview Content with
Caylen Santos

Tell us a little bit about you, your background, and your time with the ministry.

I have been married for 10 years to the most wonderful man! Mitch and I live in Nashville, TN with our Goldendoodle, Winston.

I have been in this field of ministry for 10 years and could literally not do what I do without the support of my husband. Working in the non-profit industry is hard, and compassion fatigue is so real! He is such a steady rock who encourages and supports me in every way from behind the scenes - a true legend! I'm grateful to have his support to be a woman in leadership. There are so many obstacles we must overcome as women in leadership already, and it's incredible to have your family in your corner fully supporting your role!

I grew up in a missionary household overseas, and it had a profound impact on my worldview. My Bachelor of Science in Communications has been a great tool, but the Lord has continued to use experiences from my past and present to open my heart and mind. He has opened just the right doors to allow me to join Him in His work! It's an honor to be involved daily in the life-changing work we see at The Shalom Foundation (TSF).

Tell us about your faith and how that ties in with TSF.

I love Jesus with my whole heart! As an organization, we are a faith-based non-profit whose goal is to be the hands and feet of Jesus. I have seen so many incredible miracles take place at my pediatric surgical center called The Moore Center - and it has grown my faith and encouraged me in my walk with the Lord. He always provides - even when we can't see Him working!

Tell us about your organization.

The Shalom Foundation exists to bring healing and hope to underprivileged children in Guatemala. We provide free, life-changing medical and nutritional care to those who need it most. For over 20 years, our donors have helped us serve Guatemala's most vulnerable. With our state-of-the-art medical facility and an incredible team of local staff, we can provide desperately needed surgeries for children under 18. Our mission is to give these kids healing through quality nutrition and health care, giving them hope for their future! Our Story: In the late 1990s, Steve Moore traveled to Guatemala on a mission trip with his church. So profoundly touched and moved by the people he met, he returned home with a new purpose. God had opened his heart to Guatemala, and he was led to start The Shalom Foundation.

Since then, we have built homes and schools, provided education sponsorships, installed clean water systems, and much more for the people of Guatemala. However, it was after meeting a young girl named Ana that the Foundation's mission became clear. While in Guatemala City, a sobbing aunt ran to him for aid. Her niece, Ana, had been caught in the crossfire of a gang fight and was hit with a stray bullet. After flying her to the U.S. to receive care, Steve was faced with the harsh realities many Guatemalan children experience. While

Ana thankfully recovered from her wounds, he knew that other children still lacked access to quality medical care. After learning more about the conditions many Guatemalan children live in, he was inspired with a clear vision for the Foundation: to provide critical medical, surgical, and nutritional care to underprivileged children living in poverty in Guatemala. Our Values: We believe everyone deserves access to high-quality care. We are committed to giving the highest quality care to our kids who visit the Moore Center, no matter what. That's why we have a "pay what you can" model for our patients that provides access to critical care no matter a family's financial situation. We believe care extends beyond the operating room. Our incredible social workers help each family work out the details - from transportation to and from the Moore Center for pre and post-operative care, to partnering with the Ronald McDonald House in Guatemala City so that these families have somewhere to stay while their child is being operated on, we make sure everything is taken care of.

We believe every child deserves the chance to have a brighter future. Quality of life means removing stigma and providing every child with the opportunity to succeed, regardless of the life they were born into. We check in on our kids and encourage them and their parents every step of the way. We believe we are called to partner for the greater good. Working and partnering with locals who understand the deeply rooted culture of Guatemala is the best way to ensure that we continue to meet the real needs of the people. No one knows the needs better than those who live and work in-country. By working together, we can provide the very best options for our patients. Together, we are stronger. Medical Mission Trips with The Moore Center include 3 fully equipped operating rooms, 5 PACU beds, 20 overnight recovery beds, a dental clinic, a pharmacy, a sterilization suite, a nurses' station, a family waiting area, and a cafeteria. Our center provides an independent space and organizational structure for visiting surgeons, local providers, and patients to coordinate operative and perioperative care. It is managed by The Shalom Foundation's local Guatemalan staff of administrators, physicians, nurses, and ancillary service personnel. These incredible staff members provide consistency in the practice that occurs at the Center as various visiting surgical teams rotate through.

The Shalom Foundation partners with medical professionals in the U.S.A. to coordinate one-week volunteer surgical mission trips (SMTs) across 10 different specialties to reach the underprivileged children of Guatemala at the Moore Center. During each trip, "SMT" personnel evaluate and help hundreds of patients through surgical procedures performed at the Moore Center. The Moore Center's English-speaking staff makes sure each mission week flows smoothly. Before each team's arrival, the Moore Center facilitates patient recruitment and all of the necessary patient logistics (transportation, food, temporary housing) so that each team can focus completely on providing medical and surgical care within their expertise. In addition to our professional team of full-time staff, the Moore Center can contract part-time staff for each surgical mission trip. Qualified local surgeons provide the proper pre-screening and appropriate follow-up care for each mission team's patients. In keeping with our mission, we believe that excellent post-operative care is one of the most important keys to a successful surgical outcome for each child!

When it comes to wellness, how has your organization stewarded the concept of Revive?

Our organization is very active in the "Revive" stage of the 4 R's! As a leader, it's always my goal to equip my team with the best tools I can to encourage their success in any role they take on. A big part of my role is mentoring my leadership team and helping them see their potential. I truly believe in the "people over profit" model, because when you invest in your team and truly take time to make sure they are on the "right seat on the bus", you create an environment for success. Success in their spiritual life, home life, and work life.

Every year, we have a Director's Retreat, where we fly in the healthiest CEOs and leaders, I know how important it is to teach the staff how to set healthy boundaries, combat imposter syndrome, and become better leaders. We also have a therapist who teaches classes every day during this retreat on the importance of being emotionally in tune with yourself, thereby becoming the healthiest version of yourself so that you can be the best for your family and staff. This therapist also teaches my directors tools that they can use with their staff and our patients, to make their experiences better at the Moore Center. For our staff, we highly encourage therapy regularly, provide group bonding activities once a quarter, and offer stipends for online or in-person courses to help them grow professionally. Above all, we strive to provide a workplace that can't be rivaled regarding health, well-being, and a "people first" approach. This has led to a REVIVAL among our staff, partners, and patients.

What do you do for fun? How do you incorporate Extraordinary Wellness into your life?

I love to travel to new places, arrange flowers and bouquets for friends, host women empowerment nights in my home, and take trips to the beach! I've become incredibly passionate over the years about focusing on creating a healthy, balanced lifestyle - incorporating work, play, AND rest into my routine is vital to sustaining a healthy lifestyle. I implement the 4 R's by consistently checking in with my mind and body, and I take the time to listen to what she needs so that I can continue being the best I can be. It's hard when you want to be a superwoman to everybody, but the truth is that we all need to implement the 4 R's in our own lives before we can be great for others.

What area of wellness do you need more of?

If there is one area I'd like to focus more on, it would be TRUE rest. I find that being completely still and quiet is difficult for me, as I am always on the move! Sometimes rest means having a dinner date with friends, or hiking a new trail, or traveling to beautiful places - but sometimes, the best thing you can do for yourself, and others, is allow yourself to truly stop, breathe, and be still. I'm still actively learning what that looks like in my life, but I've found that float therapy has been key for me personally to implement that kind of "still and peaceful rest".

Forefront Experience
~ Rachel Livingston

Disciple-Making Catalyst
www.forefrontexperience.com

Mission: We exist to catalyze disciple-making movements among the unreached in North America that multiply to the ends of the earth until disciples have been made of all nations.

Rachel and I have been cross-culture Kingdom 'partners in crime' since college. We had the unique privilege of being a part of the first few Passion Conferences, and while attending Oklahoma Baptist University, we had a class with Jeff Lewis, author of God's Heart for the Nations. Jeff will never know how instrumental he was in helping shape both of our hearts and minds. Like many college students at the time and since, Jeff stirred within us a heightened awareness of the Church's part, our part, in making disciples of 'all nations.' Together and in our living rooms, Rachel and I have started non-profits, served overseas, coordinated Perspectives.org courses, and led discipleship groups in many different homes and nations. I can't think of anyone more seasoned to talk about disciple-making movements in and among the unreached, and her ministry at Forefront will empower you to join God's heart for the nations, right here in our communities throughout the US!

~ TLC

Interview Content with
Rachel Livingston

Tell us a little bit about you, your background, and your time with the ministry.

I have been serving in some capacity for over 25 years. When I was in college, I read Keith Green's Last Days Ministry newsletters that I found at my parents' house. His very last newsletter was a challenge to surrender your life to the mission field. And that's what I did. Really it was surrendering to whatever God wanted for my life. I just wanted to be used for His glory! The next year I got involved in the International Student Union to welcome those studying from abroad, building friendships and sharing my life with them. I also had the opportunity to teach English in Asia for two summers and fell in love with what I got to be a part of there. That changed the trajectory of my "so-called plan" in exchange for God's plan. It led me on a path to teaching full-time in the States at a school for international students (though I initially pursued teaching overseas). God clearly wanted me here. Our school included many refugees from war-torn countries and so I found myself growing in compassion and as an advocate for the least of these and the nations God had brought to my own backyard. I had always hoped to one day be able to devote myself in a more intentional way to cross-cultural ministry. Little did I know it would be right here in the area I grew up!

I married later in life and I've only been married for just over three years. In college, I had asked the Lord to use my singleness for His purposes. I just had no idea how long that would be! My husband and I met and married in our early 40s and had our son about two years ago. Needless to say, it has been an adjustment! Particularly in the area of ministry. Single and childless for over 40 years, I was able to devote myself in a unique way to serving God. And I'm so grateful for that. Now (as it should be and as Paul tells us), my time is more divided. I'm kind of unique in my organization in that I'm the only wife and mother on staff whose husband is not on staff as well. Yet he is a wonderful support and my greatest cheerleader! Occasionally, we get to help families together, but often we pray together as a way to join in ministry.

Now that I'm a mom, it provides another connecting point for me with the women I'm seeking to minister to. I love that my child will grow up being exposed to cultures other than his own and hopefully will gain God's perspective on the nations as well.

Tell us about your faith and how that ties in with Forefront.

I grew up attending a Baptist church as a youth. Throughout the Bible, God calls us to protect and provide for the needy and the foreigner. And Jesus's last command was to go and make disciples of all nations. I have asked the Lord to break my heart for the things that break His. This is His heart. I simply desire to be obedient.

Tell us about your organization.

Billions of people cannot still hear about Jesus. An estimated three billion people around the world at this moment have little or no access to a saving relationship with Jesus. They will likely live and die without ever being introduced to the Savior of the world unless a follower of Jesus crosses a barrier to make disciples. These people are unreached.

Our organization seeks to reach the unreached living in North America. There are a number of non-profit agencies that send people overseas for cross-cultural ministry - and that is extremely important! However, our niche is to reach the unreached nations that God has brought to our door here in the United States. We see this as incredibly strategic as we do not face the same obstacles as many people living overseas. Our three main areas of focus are Outreach, Training, and Prayer.

We connect by addressing the practical needs of those we serve, often assisting families in adapting to life here in North America. We help furnish apartments, fill out forms, or take them to appointments. Another way is through teaching English and Citizenship classes. Something that can't be underestimated is simply being their friend. This is probably one of their greatest needs! Ultimately we desire to build friendships and find people of peace who are spiritually hungry. If someone expresses interest in spiritual things, we offer the chance to participate in a Discovery Bible Study where we read stories of the Bible together. We rely on the Holy Spirit as the primary teacher as we facilitate by asking simple questions. In addition, we provide training through Missional Learning Teams for people desiring to grow and be supported in how to minister cross-culturally.

It's no surprise that when people are isolated in ministry burnout and discouragement are almost guaranteed. When people are in teams, this is much less likely as it provides a natural support system for prayer, encouragement, and counsel. That's what we want to offer people seeking to do this work. Lastly, we seek to multiply extraordinary prayers. I've heard it said that we don't pray before we work, prayer is the work! Without it, we are only going in our own strength. Without a movement of prayer, we won't see a movement of God. It's critical! *By "Unreached", we are referring to those particular people groups that live/come from areas of the world that have little to no access to the gospel message and whose population is less than 2% followers of Jesus.

How do you incorporate the 4Rs of Extraordinary Wellness as an organization?

One of our core values as an organization is holistic health and being an emotionally healthy disciple. We can't pour from an empty cup! Prioritizing our relationship with Him and abiding in The Vine comes before everything else. Weekly, we gather in small teams to worship, pray, and share struggles and victories. Monthly, we dedicate at least half a day alone with God to restore our spirit and gain strength. Annually, we gather as a staff to retreat, enjoy each other, reignite vision, and grow in discipleship principles. With that being said, this season of being still a fairly new mom, the 4 R's don't come easy! Participating in these activities is a fight sometimes, but I do my best to keep showing up. I would say re-establishing regular rhythms to rejuvenate my spirit has been my goal this past year. Be it gathering weekly for team prayer, bible study, or Sunday worship - these corporate settings have been soul-nourishing, helping me fix my eyes on eternal things versus only the demands of the temporary.

What area of wellness do you need more of?

I would say "Revive." There is a lot of pouring out and when I try to replenish, it tends to replenish my body, spirit, or emotions, via rest and rejuvenation, but the sharpening of my mind is often neglected. So much vies for its attention, especially the mind-numbing scrolling of social media and all its rabbit trails! I look forward to intentionally stepping into the Revive part of the cycle.

Bless Your Heart

Faux Pas' and embarrassing or tactless acts or remarks in the crazy social situations we find ourselves!

// Celery Juice, Essential Oils, & The Magic Patch //

|| By Shari Walker ||

"When I was told I had only three weeks to live, our 12-year-old football player AJ said, "Ta, you're a fighter, it will be ok." He gave me a little penny with the cut-out of a cross that I had previously given to him, and he said, "I don't really think it's lucky, and I know it won't fix you, but it can remind you that I love you." Out of the mouth of babes!

~ AJ & TLC

****WARNING -** Some comments could be seen as snarky, cheeky, and/or offensive, read at your own risk!

Why is it that everyone becomes a doctor when they find out you have a chronic disease? I've heard it all…

- **Bee Sting Therapy -** This is when you allow bees to sting you in a controlled environment. It's supposed to help with stability and fatigue. Ummm…I'll remain unstable and tired…thank you.

- **Celery Juice Shots** - Celery juice is a miracle elixir. It will rebuild your central nervous system while flushing out toxins. Not as severe as bee stings, but anecdotal at best. There is some truth to the body flushing, fair warning!

- **Essential Oils** - Now, I'm not opposed to sitting in my favorite chair with a book next to a diffuser. It's an excellent opportunity to rest and reset. However, the claims of some of the more zealous essential oil peddlers might border on "snake oil" rather than promoting simple health benefits.

This brings me to the most recent claim for a cure…The Miracle Patch (I'll refrain from using any actual names because you know…I don't want to get sued). And if something helps increase your well-being, I'm all for it, but it's the "secret cure you HAVE to try because it will fix everything!" that gives me pause, concern and a bit of a "bless your heart!"

One day, I was leaving my office for the day. To paint a more vivid picture, it was late afternoon in the heat of summer. I was tired from staring at a computer all day, so making the walk, aided by a cane, down the hallway and to the parking lot was slow and laborious. As I was approaching my car, I heard a voice behind me. A man's voice…an unknown man's voice…asking me why I was using a cane.

I had three choices:

1. *I could whip around using my cane like a bat.*

2. *Ignore the question and continue to the car*

3. *Stop walking, answer the question, and engage in the conversation.*

First, let's be real, option #1 only happens when I daydream. I chose option #3...why did I choose option #3?!...it should never be option #3!! But I guess, I got a good story out of it.

Anyway, I told this complete stranger that I have MS, and it has affected my balance, so I use a cane when I walk. He then says, "I've got something that will help you." and launches into a long explanation of how a simple patch activates stem cells by exposing the skin to wavelengths of light. It's all-natural (it is always all-natural), super safe, and the benefits are exponential. Now I'm looking for a quick way to end this conversation so I can get home. I thanked him for his concern and asked if there was a website or if he had any material, he could give me, and I would "look into it."

Seriously, why didn't I choose option #2?!

He said, "Wait, you need to talk to my wife. She knows so much more about the product and can explain how it works better than I can." Enter the wife, or as I like to call her, The Sleeper Cell. She told me about the doctor who developed the patch and how he wanted to make it readily available to the public and bypass all the red tape from the FDA and medical community.

(Can you say red flag? Go ahead, say it with me, "Red. Flag." Good now you're getting it. 100% they were well-meaning, but bless your heart, I'm exhausted & just want to get home!)

She then said something I'd heard before: "Let me give you a free sample. If you like it, you have my contact info to get more." Now, I've never used or bought illegal drugs, but I've seen plenty of drug deals go down…on TV and in movies…and this seems to be the classic line drug pushers use on potential users. I thanked her for the sample (I'm just trying to leave), told her I would run all this by my neurologist (never did that), and would give her an update in a couple of weeks (haven't spoken to her since).

Show Up and Shut Up

One thing I have learned from all the hundreds of home remedies and MLM miracle drugs offered to me is that well-meaning folks want to step into your space, often uninvited, and give you their advice on how to remove the pain and have a better life. Again, well-meaning, bless their hearts, but most of the time, what is really needed is simple and less convenient.

Individuals dealing with sorrow, loss, pain, or suffering need a listening ear and the presence of others. The ministry of presence is powerful!

Bless their hearts, they simply need to show up and shut up.

// Mom Mishaps //

|| By Emily Bryant ||

"Nothing says 'Growth Mindset' like a Trip of a Lifetime to Spain and a head full of Lice!"

It was the fall of 2022. My children had grown so much. I now had an 8th-grade son, a 6th-grade daughter, a 3rd-grade daughter, and a 4-year-old in Pre-K. Sports for my oldest had really picked up this year, and we found ourselves at soccer games most weekends, football games many weeknights, and after-school activities most afternoons. Life was busier than ever, and this mom was overwhelmed.

Don't get me wrong, I was truly grateful for everything and every one of my kids, wait... no, yeah, every one of them! But, I was really struggling with being a happy mom. I wanted to be joyful and fun for my family, but often found myself too grumpy, short-tempered, and exhausted. Like anyone. I had a good day sneak in there every so often, but it just seemed that the hard days were trying to take over! I knew I needed a change.

The truth was, I realized that something in me needed to change. I had to find a way to reconnect with God, to anchor back to him, and to find his strength where I was lacking. One afternoon, I was scrolling through Facebook, and stumbled across an ad that gave me pause: "Family Journey: Slowing-down, connecting, radical self-care, real rest and regeneration." WOW! They had me at radical self-care. SIGN ME UP! I quickly messaged the owner, Evan, and began to ask some questions. What he was offering were family trips that seemed to line up perfectly with what I was seeking.

He taught meditation and helped families reach a more grounded space to face their challenges. It took some coaxing, but I eventually got James on board to take a trip with Family Journey. We were going to Spain in the summer of 2023, and we were going to seek radical change! We knew we were crazy to sign up for a trip through a Facebook ad, but good things come to those who take risks, right? We prayed about it and leaned into God, trusting that he had a plan for us. Little did I know, we were not only taking a risk by going on this trip, but we were also embarking on another type of journey: LICE. Yes, lice. As in the bug that lives on your scalp. My middle daughter briefly mentioned that her head itched before we left on the trip, and I simply stated that she needed to quit skipping her showers. Solid parenting advice I might add! "When our heads are dirty, they can be itchy!" Duh! Small humans!

Since we were traveling far from Texas, we decided to book our trip for two weeks.

The first week we would spend on our own, and the second week we would join Evan and his family for the Family Journey.

The first week was full of exciting new things like driving in Europe, taking the metro, staying in strange and cool Air B&Bs, taking a family hike through their beautiful country, exploring a castle or two, and going to the balloon museum! Who ever knew there was such a thing?

After the first week and second town, we arrived at our third location for the Family Journey portion of the trip. We were exhausted, and my daughter was a bit itchier, seriously... like shower already! We were supposed to meet our host family that evening, and I had become increasingly concerned about the itchy head my daughter was complaining about. I mean, I saw her take a shower, so if it was lice, I didn't want to bring it to our host family! I combed through my daughter's hair, but I didn't see anything. Out of an abundance of caution, we pushed through our fatigue and drove to the local pharmacy. Upon arrival, we Googled "lice" in Spanish, and bought the only box of lice treatment that the small store had. I couldn't read the directions, so I wasn't sure if it would kill any potential eggs. "That's OK", I thought to myself. If it is lice, we can treat the bugs here, and kill any eggs back home in the States.

So, it was time for dinner, and we still had not treated her hair. So, I fixed it and threw a ball cap on her suspicious head before we went to our host home to meet them, for the first time I might add. Like any good parent, I pushed the thought of lice out of my head for the evening and had a delightful dinner with this family.

It was going to be a good week!

After dinner, we went back, and I proceeded to treat my daughter's hair instead of going to bed. Honestly, y'all, I was so tired, sleep was calling my name, but I let the solution soak and began the comb out. To my utter horror, I began combing dead bugs out of my daughter's hair–not just a few, like an entire village of dead bugs.

No question at this point, she definitely had lice, and it wasn't a mild case. My mind swirled with questions: "Did they jump on our host Evan's kids? Can lice jump? Wait... Do I have lice?! Do WE have lice? Are they on the couch? Oh no... are they in our family hairbrush?" You get the idea. At this point, all I could do was finish the treatment and pass out.

For the rest of the trip, we were pretty sure we had the lice under control and tried not to think about lice. We wanted to take full advantage of the time, so we did!

I focused on learning how to meditate, how to reach Jesus through this meditation, and was moved to tears at His glory. James and I were also coached on parenting, and Evan helped us work through some family kinks. We learned so much, and our cups were full! Ironically, MY head was itching a little bit. I kept telling myself it was psychosomatic, but I insisted that James check my head five times a day. Each time, he would painstakingly look through my hair and tell me to stop worrying, "You don't have lice! It's fine!" Whew!

So, there we were on a 10-hour plane ride home when I realized that my head was on fire! It was like a whole new level of itchiness. I also discovered some small, interesting bumps on the base of my neck and hairline. I asked James to look at these, and he replied by saying, "Weird. It looks like you have acne on your neck." Yep, I knew at that moment that those were bug bites. I glanced across the aisle at my kids all sitting together, and pictured tiny lice playing red-rover and tag, all over their heads, the plane, and all those unassuming innocent passengers on the plane! I was horrified. Again.

If you have ever had children come home from school with lice, then you will understand what comes next! The next two MONTHS involved buying drugstore lice products, treating the lice with said products, and finding lice on everyone except James (he is bald - lucky!). Daily combing, treating, combing, shaking my head, crying a tad, and combing some more. After treating everyone twice and finding lice on someone AGAIN, I decided to call in the big guns: The lice clinic. That's right, there's a clinic for this! They are the professional lice killers of the community! At the clinic, they informed me that lice have evolved since we were kids, but the products have not. Apparently, the bugs got smarter, but the people have not! The product SAYS it kills the lice eggs, but they lie! Come to find out, lice must be frozen off or combed out one by one, and if you missed one, too bad for you. They are coming back with a vengeance... mean little bugs! Five treatments and $1000 later we were lice-free! Finally! Until we were not. Seriously?!

The clinic promised to stick with us until we were free of those pesky rogue lice! Eventually, we were free. And finally, they were really gone.

It's funny how often we think we have everything under control and choose not to have a growth mindset because we don't see any bugs, I mean problems. Yet, if we would just choose to get tools along the way, we would be better equipped to address problems when they arise. If fact, if we would choose to learn new tools, before we need them, it might just save us extensive head-itches, I mean headaches, in the long run. I love how God will use even lice to bring a growth mindset and to bring families together!

Ironically, it sounds like lice have their own growth mindset and have found ways to evolve!

Even as I write this, I wonder if they're back.

Oh man, I think my head is itching!

// It's True, I Heard it Once! //

|| By Ann Sullivan ||

See You at the Pole |

Leaving on a jet plane. Don't know when I'll be back again…literally!

A few years ago, my husband, Bill, was working on an assignment for a construction project in Des Moines, Iowa, while I was working at a hospital in Florida. We had planned to meet in Columbia, South Carolina for my cousin's wedding and a weeklong celebration for my mom's 70th birthday. Because we were starting our week in Columbia, SC but ending our weeklong excursion in Savannah, GA, I had to be sure to triangulate my husband's flight details.

My parents, grandmother & I were all traveling by vehicle and were planning to meet him the day before the wedding in South Carolina. My husband went to the airport in Des Moines with anticipation of meeting us in Columbia, unfortunately, the airline had a computer glitch nationwide which grounded all flights for the evening.

Bill decided to return to his hotel and would attempt to take the same flight the following day. Because of the timing of Bill's arrival in Columbia, it would mean he would unfortunately miss my cousin's wedding all together. Near the end of the reception, I checked his flight status and drove to the airport to pick up my husband. The airport in Columbia is small and therefore, I was able to watch the takeoff and landing of each flight.

As I was sitting in my car, scrolling through my phone, Bill texted me to say that he had landed and was waiting out front of the terminal "by the flagpole". I gingerly pulled up the 100+ yards to the front of the terminal and to my dismay, I didn't see Bill or a flagpole. My heart sank, and I began to check the "Find My Friend" app to see the location of my husband. There he was! "Whew!" on the app, it showed him standing right in front of the Columbia airport... Unfortunately, as I zoomed out, my stomach turned because I realized the location of my husband's icon was in the middle of the United States... he was definitely at the Columbia airport... unfortunately, it was at the Columbia, Missouri airport. I immediately called him to profusely apologize and sort out the confusion.

Needless to say, he was tired and frustrated by the outcome. But we're still married, we'll count that a win! We ultimately rebooked him on a third flight in which he met us in Charleston, SC the following day. To this day, retelling this story provides my entire family with so much joy and laughter. We often end conversations with "See you at the flagpole".

Let this also serve as a warning to those who would ask me to make their travel arrangements.

God's Got You
We'll Walk with You
You've Got This!

Practical Applications

Tools, devotions, journals, and prayers to help you tap into your privilege as a child of God, use your gorgeous guidebook, the Bible, step into your trusted Code Grape Tribe, and experience Extraordinary Wellness in your everyday!

// By: Natalyia Rutherford //

CONFESSION TIME.

Revival does not come naturally to me.

I guess it's a by-product of being easily contented. Find pleasure and joy in simple things? Some other really nice way to spin it? Goal setting and time management, all of that takes extra work for me. My husband, the ever-patient man he is, has made the joke that I am very "godly". The first time I thought "How sweet!" and was expecting some insightful compliment... and then he went on to say, "In the sense that time holds no meaning for you." (Insert eye roll.) I'd like to say it was the one time, but it continues occasionally with "there you go being godly again". Ha! But he's not wrong. It's not my strength and so you may be thinking why am I writing this section? Well, because it takes extra work and because I DO want to improve, I've done quite a bit of research on it. So, if you do well at this - hopefully you will still find a few new ideas. If this doesn't come naturally, know you're not alone. I'll always be working on this right along with you!

I love how John Piper, in an interview with "Desiring God", describes revival*. "The idea of revival originates in the reality that, on the one hand, God is the decisive giver of all spiritual life and, on the other hand, humans, even those who are born again and part of God's covenant family, from time-to-time drift into a kind of lifelessness and lethargy and backsliding and indifference and weakness. And when you put those two together – God as the giver of life and man as ever drifting towards lifelessness – what you get is the need for the hope of reviving, coming back to life – a fresh outpouring of God's life-giving Spirit on his people. That is what revival is." Of course, we're going to take it a little further. We are to live this revival in all areas of our life right? So, let's dig in and see how we can revive the different parts of our lives to His glory.

Revival Tools: All self-improvement has to begin with self-knowledge. There are many tools Tonya listed out at the beginning of this section and it's a really comprehensive list of assessment tools. I LOVE a good personality quiz. There is much to learn about ourselves through them, here are just a few: Myers Briggs, DISC, the SDI, Color Personality, and Enneagram. It's also interesting to see how your family members or co-workers test and see how you all balance and work together. If you have the time to do one, I recommend you do that now.

If you don't have time, or if you have done them already, here are a few questions to get your brain going:

- What are your values?

- What are your motivators?

- What are your energy needs? *(look at your daily routine, when you have the most focus, work needs, rest needs - daily, monthly, yearly)*

- **List your natural preferences** *(learning style, strengths & abilities, personality, emotional intelligence, source of confidence)*

____
____
____
____
____
____

- **What holds you back?** *(fears, unhealthy desires, cravings, and expectations)*

____
____
____
____
____
____

Whether you completed the questions above or completed an online assessment tool, kudos to you! Bonus points if you get input/feedback from someone close to you. How others see us can definitely clue us into parts of ourselves we don't see (not just negatively, but positively too). I hope this gives you a clearer starting point.

Next is goal setting, or my favorite word for it - vision casting. I personally feel "goal setting" has been overused and has earned a big ol' BLEH from me. I prefer vision casting because it gets me excited and sounds so magical - even if it's just block-scheduling my home cleaning/organizing.

I think most of us know the SMART method for setting goals (specific, measurable, achievable, relevant, and time-bound). We'll be using this across the areas of our life but again, don't feel stressed to fill out every section. Pick areas you're ready to tackle. Goals, or visions, should continue to be reassessed. Tackle what is realistic and attainable for now. You can always come back and do a new one when you're ready to do more!

Personally

(internal goals: mental health, physical, financial, spiritual)

Specific	
Measurable	
Achievable	
Relevant	
Time Bound	

Home

Specific	
Measurable	
Achievable	
Relevant	
Time Bound	

Work

Specific	
Measurable	
Achievable	
Relevant	
Time Bound	

Community

Specific	
Measurable	
Achievable	
Relevant	
Time Bound	

Wow, this is some good work you're doing here!

However, if that just left you feeling a little mentally exhausted... that's not what we're going for here.

Give yourself permission to have a little fun with this!

We all know that writing things out by hand increases the likelihood you'll remember, and you just did that. I highly recommend taking this and creating something to get you excited and keep your focus on these goals! My sister creates beautiful vision boards, and it inspired me to have the kids in my support groups do the same. It's amazing to see how each one is uniquely revealing and exciting. I wanted to make mine easy to remember so I put it into an acrostic "DREAMS" - devotionals, relationships, exploration, ambition, money, and strength. It's based off of Eleanor Roosevelt's quote "The future belongs to those who believe in the beauty of their DREAMS. Or it can be as simple as putting Post-its up on your mirror! Take a creative break and get yourself excited about these goals you worked so hard on!

"These commandments that I give you today are to be on
your hearts. Impress them on your children. Talk about
them
when you sit at home and when you walk along the road,
when you lie down and when you get up. Tie them as
symbols on your hands and bind them on your
foreheads. Write them on the door
frames of your houses and
on your gates."
~ Deut. 6:6-9

Ok, you're back! Now that you're ready to tackle these beautiful goals you set, let's talk about what tools you'll need to accomplish them.

Internal Tools:

It's only right that we start with God first!

1. What spiritual tools will you use to help yourself achieve these goals?

____
____
____
____
____
____

Ideas: try a centering prayer, breath work, chakras, liturgies, or fasting

2. Which of your above goals are you most excited to learn more about? List some apps, books, or tools that will help you achieve that goal:

____
____

3. **What routines can you create that will help you engage with your goals?** I love habit stacking and time blocking but seriously, if you Google time management tools, it's a never-ending list BUT that means there's something for everyone! Create your routine in the block below, or on a separate piece of paper. (Bonus Tip… And then take a picture to keep it handy so you can remember!)

4. **What about the internal narration you have going on?** We've done a lot of work listing affirmations and bible verses in the past sections, but it deserves a second look. If you haven't already, make a plan now of how you will limit ANY negative self-talk. I personally like having 3 scriptures on my Keep app. When those negative voices start creeping in, I open that app and read and meditate on that. Once those are committed to memory, I add three new ones.

Engagement Tools:

1. There isn't enough out there on accountability and its benefits. I strongly believe in it but don't always make time for it as I should. Confession and accountability with God is a type of worship that yields AMAZING benefits that reverberate throughout the areas of my life. When I do it well, I feel more intimate with Him. I am more thankful and aware of what He's done daily in my life. I am more gracious toward others, and MYSELF, in failings. How can you practice accountability with God in the goals that you've set?

2. I also believe God has placed a select group of people in our lives that we can place accountability with. Who in your circle can you trust to be honest with you? Who is your problem solver? Who is your cheerleader? These might all be different people and that's ok! List them all here:

"Iron sharpens iron, and one man sharpens another."

~ Prov. 27:17

"Whoever walks with the wise becomes wise, but the companion of fools will suffer harm."

~ Prov. 13:20

"Without counsel plans fail, but with many advisers they succeed."

~ Prov. 15:22

Can you tell me where I'm going with this?

Mentors!

Every successful person achieving their goals has mentors who have helped them along the way. Anthony Tjan**, CEO of Cue Ball Group, lists a few types of mentors to look for in your circle below:

1. The master of the craft - the best in your field. They can help identify, realize, and hone your strengths and share their wisdom and experience as well.

2. The champion of your cause - your connector. They believe in you and will want to connect you to others who may believe in what you do.

3. The co-pilot - your best work bud. They are someone you can bounce ideas off of, listen to you vent, and collaborate with you.

4. The anchor - friend or family member. This person keeps your best interests in mind and can help set priorities and life balance.

5. The reverse mentor - we can learn from mentees as well. They give us feedback on our leadership style and keep our perspective fresh and relevant.

List below those that fit the above descriptions and see if they would be willing to be a mentor and meet with you a couple of times through the year.

____

____

____

____

____

____

Proverbs 4:25-26 25

Let your eyes look straight ahead;

fix your gaze directly before you. 26 Give careful thought to the paths for your feet and be steadfast in all your ways the idea of revival originates in the reality that, on the one hand, God is the decisive giver of all spiritual life and, on the other hand, humans, even those who are born again and part of God's covenant family, from time-to-time drift into a kind of lifelessness and lethargy and backsliding and indifference and weakness. And when you put those two together – God as the giver of life and man as ever drifting towards lifelessness – what you get is the need for the hope of reviving, coming back to life – a fresh outpouring of God's life-giving Spirit on his people. That is what revival is."

PRAYER OF REVIVAL

Heavenly Father,

I praise You as the giver of all spiritual life, everlasting life. I confess I minister out of emptiness at times. I drift into lifelessness and apathy after denying myself rest in You, forgetting the joy I have in knowing You are God, and I am not. Thank you for calling me back to you Lord and awakening my passion again. Thank you for the people and opportunities you place in my life to continue my growth and my purpose.

Father, please give me a spirit of wisdom and refresh my zeal to love and serve the world You came to save.

Amen!

- https://www.desiringgod.org/interviews/what-is-revival-and-where-do-we-find-it
- https://ideas.ted.com/the-5-types-of-mentors-you-need-in-your-life/

Chapter Five

Relaunch Culture

RELAUNCH |
Rethinking a Biblical Approach to Relaunch

In this section, we are looking at all of the stories and information through the lens of **RELAUNCHING** well. Extraordinary Wellness uses the following acronym to help us understand, plan for, and apply 'RELAUNCH' into our daily lives.

ReLAUNCH | Scripture: Isaiah 6:8-13

"Then I heard the voice of the Lord saying, "Who shall I send and who will go for us? And I said, 'Here I am; send me!"

Definition: Stepping into ministry, re-engaging into your sphere of influence. Once you've rested, rejuvenated, and learned something through a new perspective, it's time to put your newfound mindset, energy, and knowledge to use!

Rethinking my ReLaunch | Going into my Sphere of Influence, with a renewed sense of mission and with an Extraordinary Wellness approach for myself & those around me.

Life Giving | Living a life that is not my own is mission-driven, for His glory, using my blessings to be a blessing, peace, and hope to those in my sphere of influence… to make disciples.

'Life-Giving' is for both me and for others. We can't pour from an empty cup/vessel. This is the difference between relational discipleship vs. performance/task-oriented.

Accountability | Are you accountable to other Believers? Are you aware that we are called to be responsible, even liable, and must give an account for our actions in this life?

That 'account' is to God the Father, but a critical component in our Christian faith is walking alongside other Believers as we sort through our relationships both horizontally, with people, and vertically with God. This can only be done with vulnerability, trust, and asking each other the hard questions. And even then, we must be willing to answer the hard questions. Our life will have an impact on those around us, our sphere of influence… our thoughts, actions, and our words matter. We need each other to walk through all stages of struggles and wellness.

Use My Tools | Evaluate which tools you need, as you encounter opportunities to use them. Do you need to use your internal tools, visible tools, adjustment tools, or language tools? Practice these tools daily, weekly, or monthly. The more you utilize them, the more they become part of your positive habits.

Navigation | Indicators Flags, taking the Pulse on the Health of myself, my family, my environment, and those in my sphere.

Connection | Set aside protected time for community and interpersonal relationships (3C Team)

Have a 4R Plan | Before scheduling your calendar and setting aside intentional time, think through your current routines & rituals. What new routines or rituals need to be created, updated, or eliminated?

1. REST
Where? ______________________________
When? ______________________________
How? ______________________________

Ponder these three questions in your plan to be successful in disconnecting with technology. What alternative plans or arrangements do you need to make so the people and business you are responsible for are taken care of? Only then can your mind, body, and spirit have a real opportunity to disconnect and rest.

2. REJUVENATE
Where? ______________________________
When? ______________________________
How? ______________________________

- *Think about the above three questions in your plan to enjoy, laugh, relax, and engage the world with wonder.*

- *What plans or arrangements do you need to make so you can truly enjoy, this is a no-stress experience.*

- *If stressed, call a mulligan and choose a different "let your hair down" experience.*

- *Remember, connecting with nature, water, exercise, games, using multiple senses, and laughter are all brilliant ways to regulate and create endorphins within your body chemistry!*

- *And if you need some funny outlets to make you laugh, see the "Bless Your Heart" or Resources sections!*

3. REVIVE

Who? ____
Where? ____
When? ____
How? ____

Think about the above four questions as you plan to gain new tools or new knowledge.

- *What do you really want or need to learn?*

- *Ask the Lord to show you a new perspective within familiar content.*

- *How could you potentially apply the new knowledge?*

4. RELAUNCH

With whom? ______________________________
Where? ______________________________
When? ______________________________
How? ______________________________
Why? ______________________________

- *When is the right time? When do you need to re-engage in your sphere of influence with intentional purpose?*

- *Where is your sphere of influence?*

- *Who is in your sphere of influence?*

- *How will you use your new tools to bless, reach, or bring wellness to them?*

- *And why? What is your why? We already know that we value people, but take a moment to think through the "why" God has placed these specific people and groups into your spaces and places of influence.*

Create a Culture of Relaunch

Think of the 'launching pad' concept when you think of the plan that God has for you according to Jeremiah 29:11. Walk with courage and your head high (Josh 1:9), because we know with absolute certainty, that He called you, and will equip you, with His Holy Spirit power to bring His presence, knowledge, and peace into the sphere of influence He has asked you to steward!

Make Relaunch Culture a Practice

A Culture of Relaunch will regularly utilize your family, your Code Grape Girls, and the Church. We were never designed to do this life alone.

- Just remember that the 4R Cycle is a period motion cycle that can go back and forth, and always with the intention of ultimately moving clockwise.

If You're Trying to Drive Me Crazy, It's Too Late!

Real Stories, Real Woman, Real Themes of Life
By: Aimee Rhodes

We are here to tell you **RELAUNCH** is achievable in all the true stories you are about to read! **There is hope!**

Single, Professional Woman

Kendra finds herself in a new office and has had much time to work on herself and recently took on a new role in her career. She was able to snag a managerial position, which has created more space for her to grow in her profession. Kendra still struggles with keeping up with her own needs but thinks being a manager will help her manage her time better than carrying a caseload. She is unsure of the idea of leading people but figures she has to try sometimes. Kendra has never really had any quality leaders to look up to until this job, so she is looking forward to learning from them and getting guidance. She feels like a fish out of water since she grew up in a blue-collar home with both her parents having had union jobs. She thinks on occasion, "I feel like an imposter being here but I'm ready to relaunch into my next steps of this greater calling."

Kendra is looking forward to having a closer relationship with her leaders and a new mentor she met at church. She wants to be able to overcome some of the barriers to being a successful manager and being relationally driven to meet the needs of her team. She sets up her office and just hopes for the best. She doesn't really know where to get started and how to develop a system that supports her maintaining her mental and physical wellness that she has newly started the journey towards.

Her desire is so strong to further this calling to open a non-profit she wants to be the best version of herself and be prepared for the challenges of starting something from the ground up. But first, she is going to focus on being a leader. Her new manager comes in and meets with Kendra and explores with her greatest desires the barriers she faces to achieve those goals. The manager quickly jots down a list of reading materials for Kendra to begin reading. She sets up a time to meet with her later in the week to determine her performance goals for the year. Kendra begins to panic and feels unsure of what she should be focusing on as a manager, after all, she hasn't been one before.

Her manager assures her she will be able to identify a couple of goals as long as she gets to reading those books. Kendra nods her head and hops into her online account to order digital books and begins the next steps into her relaunch journey. She grits her teeth but figures she can at least start with one book and work her way down the list.

Living with Chronic Illness/Terminal Illnesses

Maya has followed up with her oncologist and determined her next steps as she has received all her chemo treatments. Maya's treatments have been all over the place, but has been making successive progress. The oncologist shares that the mass is reducing in size and does not appear to be attached or wrapped around any of her vital organs.

Maya has been asking for regular help from her friends for a few things but also was able to get someone to come help with light housekeeping. This has been a weight off of Maya's shoulders as she has navigated trying new things for her overall well-being. She has been following the doctor's recommendations with supplements, and nutritional shakes to help add more nutrition to her regular meals. Maya braces as she asks the oncologist about her prognosis for returning to her career.

He gently smiles and says "Maya, I think you can return but you have to promise to take it slow and keep your stress level down. While you have done well with chemo you will have to maintain certain treatments along the way so that we can get the mass even smaller.". Maya looks wide-eyed but hopeful as she has worked diligently at following protocols, tried some new things and even got back into her workouts but at a much slower pace.

Maya longs to start back and tackle the projects that were put on hold for her. The doctor reminds her a second time to take it easy and only to work part-time to reduce stressors. Maya nods her head and texts her boss to let them know she will be returning part-time.

Maya returns home and shares the news with her husband, who has been with her the entire way. He is happy for her as he knows her true passion in life is her projects in her corporate training job. He encourages her to take it slow and that he will keep an eye out on her to ensure she isn't overdoing it. Maya, who has been off work for a while, now feels like she has to catch up on where the company is and get a lay of the land so they can begin developing the programs. She isn't even sure who remains on the team it's been so long, so she sets out to meet with her leader and discuss the status and who she can depend on to help launch things.

Maya is hopeful but somewhat hesitant about who will be in her corner when it comes to work but knows she has a good community with friends to help hold her accountable for both her physical well-being and enjoying the things she loves. She's hesitant but she's ready to relaunch and return to the giftings she has.

Mamahood, from Littles to Hormonal Teenagers

Fatima takes a break from her work as she recently was able to find a part-time job to further her career. They were able to be flexible with her and allow her to work from home and provide virtual meetings with clients. Fatima has tapped into asking for help from her husband and mother-in-law for a couple of mornings and an evening a week to get the timeslots blocked. Fatima wants to remain present for her children, so she chose times they would be out at a half-day program where they get to socialize with kids her age. Fatima will still have the baby with her but he's a quiet one for now and can take breaks to nurse him between meetings.

Fatima shared that she is very grateful for her mother-in-law coming at the right time and the family's commitment to supporting each other as well as Fatima's career path. They all have mentioned that they know the kids won't be this small very long and part-time works really well for everyone involved. With the kids now being in a day program it has given Fatima time to have a peaceful shower or use the restroom in peace. They still sit in her lap at dinner, but Fatima doesn't mind so much knowing she has some alone time to work, talk to other adults, and achieve her goals.

Fatima is unsure how the work will go but is eager to learn the skills it takes to be fully certified. She finds she is less tired, and less irritable and feels like she can be a good mother now. She was amazed at the improvement the small breaks had in her mood. She even found time to take an intensive training program online. She hopes to use this, plus her supervisor's support, to take her to the next level. She waits and waits as one does when you do referral-based work. But she is excited as she takes on her first client. Her ability to apply the skills she has learned finally came into practice to help a real-life person.

Fatima reaches out to her friend with the teens once again and finds that the friend is making progress as well. She has found her own rest, hobbies and has taken time to reconnect with her support system. Fatima's friend has been able to make peace with the outcome of her teen's behaviors and was thankful that those in charge were more lenient to give her a chance to help her kids finally get the skills to not repeat the same mistakes. Fatima shares the teens are pretty scared to return to poor behavior and have cleaned up their act for the time being. Fatima offers a prayer with her friend of protection for her teens who try her nerves.

Living Life with Older Parents in Late Stages of Life

Charlene, with the support of her siblings and her husband, has made the final decision to place her mother and father in a supportive community that can help with the mother's dementia but also maintain her independence as long as possible. Charlene shares the community offers many amenities that will engage her parents in community, social activities, physical activity, and even help provide transportation to stores for the essentials. Charlene was able to take the breaks recommended and find time to visit her parents again a couple of times a week. She does not feel pressured to take control of their care anymore but trusts the professionals she has hired to help.

Charlene, while she has to continue to face the fact her mother's health will not get better, can be present during their time together and has begun to help her make end-of-life decisions while her mother still has lucid moments. Charlene has been able to be rested, and relaxed, which has helped her relationship with her mother and father. They have been able to play games and watch movies together on the weekends and during the week share a meal.

Charlene has taken time to herself before she resumes the work world, giving her time to create healthy patterns of living and heal the fallout of burnout. Charlene was able to resume some lost hobbies and make a few friends when time permitted. Charlene is finally hopeful to be able to minister to her parents in their time of life while also finding enjoyment in her daily work.

Each of these women has worked hard in their journey to be ready to RELAUNCH into their fields of influence.

Whether it be their work, children, parents, ministry, or their health. They are prepared to access their resources, including the Code Grape women in their sphere, so they can live extraordinarily for the Kingdom of God.

Hope is here… it's time to take steps, in faith!

- It begins with the recognition of the need and practice of rest.
- Choosing joy may have seemed like a difficult practice at first, but it's amazing how it changes perspective.
- Once there is breathing space and the ability to absorb new information with a clear head, gaining tools is inevitable!
- And then, watch out world, because God's chosen are now rested up, freed up, and equipped to change the atmosphere around them!

I'm Over 40 and I Know Some Stuff Now!

Chats with Specialists in their Fields.

Ann Sullivan

Paradise Has Its Own Issues!

Physician Assistant & Disciple

How do you describe Annie? She's the human equivalent to laughter! She IS the ministry of presence... Joy in human form, with the passion and courage to take the joy into the darkest of places! I have had the honor of living and traveling with Annie off and on for around 20 years... from the POC in Texas, to Africa, Europe, and the Middle East, we've had more laughter in the most dangerous of places... Truly, Annie is a gift to all who know her! She is like the walking version of laughing gas, no matter how difficult or precarious the moment may seem, she will bring reprieve to the weariest of souls, just by being present!

~ TLC

Growing up in the Midwest, we only traveled as far west as St Louis, far east as Columbus, OH, as far north as Chicago & as far south as Tennessee. I truly thought it was "too far" to go past this circumference centralized around Illinois and Indiana. God has knocked my socks off in the last 25 years leading & guiding me to live, work, and serve all over the world including Thailand, Honduras, Guatemala, Kenya, Liberia, St Croix US Virgin Islands, and so many others. He has continued to ask us to use our God-given talents to serve others. Because of this continual surrender and living palms up, my husband & I have moved a lot when God has asked us to hold things loosely, downsize, purge our belongings, pack up the rest & move to the next location for our next "assignment". Living in such a way has been life-altering and life-giving!! The Lord continues to engage us and relaunch us into our next sphere of influence.

When I truly surrendered my life to Christ 25 years ago, I knew at that moment that I had received the Holy Spirit. However, I didn't know exactly what that entails. I can honestly say that I am still learning new ways that the Lord speaks to me. Approximately 10 years ago, the Lord moved my husband and I to the US Virgin Islands. Living on a Caribbean Island sounds like a dream. However, let me be honest, "paradise" has its own issues including drugs, violence, racism, nepotism, and poverty to name a few.

During our stint on the island, we experienced the Kingdom of God/Family of God profoundly. Our church family consisted of approximately 200 people representing 20+ nationalities and at times, worshiping in different languages. To us, this was what the "Family of God" should feel like and look like. This experience made me feel at home but with eager anticipation of heaven on earth. After being on the island for approximately 2 years, neither of us was planning on moving off the island. In fact, we both thought we heard the Lord prompting us to stay and purchase a home on the island. My husband has vast experience in the construction industry.

While surveying homes on the island that were available for purchase, we realized they did not meet stateside construction standards and quite often were "jerry-rigged". Despite this lack of standard, we continued to walk out of our faith and continued to search for a home. During this process, one day my husband and I were sitting side by side on the couch in our 1-bedroom apartment. I was researching available island homes on MLS websites when I heard a still small voice say "Consider moving stateside".

Obviously, this was a jolt to my system as Bill and I thought the Lord was prompting us to stay on the island. Without saying a word, I quietly closed my laptop and sat in the stillness of our living room. I prayed, "Lord, if this is you, I need you to confirm what you just said." Without prompting, Bill turned to me and said "I just had the strangest thought. We should consider moving stateside." We knew at that moment, that it was time for us to resign from our jobs, pack up our belongings and return to the States as the Lord was definitely 'relaunching' us into our next chapter.

Tonya Lincoln

<u>I'm not dead yet!</u>

Diplomat, Non-Profiteer Teacher, Tata, Babes, & Chick-a-Pee.

Authentically and unapologetically herself, that's how I would describe Tonya. I think in a world littered with hidden agendas; this is an unusually refreshing characteristic. Ironically, because it is rare, it can also be misunderstood, I'm here to attest, that she actually means it, whatever 'it' is! I met Tonya around 20+ years ago at Cambridge. I have been her professor, a chair on her committee, & her employer for many international educational projects, and I'm proud to say her friend. She has looked death in the face without fear on several occasions, and she speaks with deep conviction. She sent me a card when my daughter was diagnosed with Stage 4 breast cancer. It simply said, "I love you, just tell me what you need, when you need it." That was it, it was all I needed to hear, and she meant it! There was a quote written in the card that said, "If you can't see His way past the tears, trust His heart." by Charles Spurgeon. It was signed, "TLC" as she always does. I'm not sure if her parents gave her those initials on purpose, but she lives them out! To me, that sums up my dear Tonya, whom I call friend.

~ Dr. Clara Sharma

What an amazing God we serve!
A God whose Word brings us Extraordinary Wellness.

I have many faces... I'm not suffering from multiple-personality disorder, at least usually (she pauses to consider the possibility) ... But I do have the honor of holding many roles and responsibilities, and each comes with a different name, set of expectations, learning curves, and growth-mindset... just like every other woman I know! Let's hear it for Venusian Spaghetti! (Shout out to John Gray and the Farrels! See the resource section!)

I know there is nothing good in me without Him, that's pretty evident to anyone who knows me. But, as I attempt to step into His righteousness, not mine, I thought I would walk through some of the names that are used to signal or identify me. I think they help embody how my magnificent God has shown-up, showed-off, and brought cycles of Extraordinary Wellness, into my world, even when I was an unwilling participant!

When we talk about relaunching, it simply means stepping into our sphere of influence, and claiming our identity and authority in Christ. There is so much rhetoric in today's culture about identity. Much of this conversation revolves around how individuals 'feel' about who they are. If we're being honest, I think as humans we have too much internal self-talk and struggle (sin), to depend on our wants and our emotions. I think the Bible is pretty clear about the condition of the human heart when left to its own devices. Don't get me wrong, there is something truly spectacular about humanity, after all, we are made in His image. But our freewill will 'literally' be the death of us if we don't give our will and life back to the Creator who handcrafted us. Scripture comes with the full story, but take a minute to review and remember who we are without Him. Romans 1:28: God gave them over to a depraved mind, to do those things which are not proper.

- **Jeremiah 17:9:** The heart is more deceitful than all else and is desperately sick; who can understand it?

- **Colossians 2:18:** Let no one keep defrauding you of your prize by delighting in self-abasement and the worship of the angels, taking his stand on visions he has seen, inflated without cause by his fleshly mind.

- **Genesis 6:5:** The Lord saw that the wickedness of man was great on the earth, and that every intent of the thoughts of his heart was only evil continually.

- **Romans 12:21:** Do not be overcome by evil but overcome evil with good.

Here's the GREAT news, He fixed it! The gospel is the great news: We are His workmanship. He loves and chooses us. We chose sin. We cannot reach a perfect state on our own. He sacrificed His perfect self for our selfish, guilty selves. We can choose His redemptive forgiveness. We can walk in His Spirit. We are adopted by Him with all the rights, titles, and authorities that come with being a child, an heir, to Jehovah God, the King of Kings.

Truth... it's not just great, it's good. Like full of goodness. This 'good news' is perfectly good because, at His core, God is good; implicitly, entirely, and without change. That means we can sincerely trust Him, even when we don't understand, or have some, let's say, trepidation. We can trust Him because He is good. Do you remember "The Lion, the Witch & the Wardrobe?" There's a line that says, "Safe?"... Who said anything about safe? 'Course he isn't safe. But he's good. He's the King, I tell you." That my friend, is a pretty good human understanding of my God, our God... The God. His very presence is so powerful it can obliterate anything in His presence. Poor Moses barely glimpsed at His backside and it seared his pupils for life. It makes sense if you think about the pure power of a being who simply spoke everything into existence! I had a friend who permanently lost sight from simply staring at the sun... can you imagine looking at the sheer magnitude of pure power, raw GOD Power?!

Again, in that regard, He is NOT safe, but He IS good! He is good. He is good. He is good. I know myself and trust me, I need Him to be the leader and Lord that guides my life. Anyone who depends on me needs me to surrender to His will and not my own.

The Good News:

- **Ephesians 2:10** - For we are his workmanship, created in Christ Jesus unto good works, which God hath before ordained that we should walk in them.

- **Romans 8:1** - There is therefore now no condemnation to them which are in Christ Jesus, who walk not after the flesh, but after the Spirit.

- **Genesis 1:27** - So, God created man in his own image, in the image of God, He created them male and female.

- **1 John 4:12** - No one has ever seen God; but if we love one another, God remains in us, and His love is perfected in us.

- **Psalm 34:8** - Taste and see that the Lord is good; blessed is the one who takes refuge in him.

- **Romans 10:9-10** - Confess with your mouth the Lord Jesus and believe in your heart that God raised him from the dead, and you will be saved.

- **Romans 10:13** - Call upon the name of the Lord and you will be saved.

- **Ephesians 2:8-10** - For by grace are ye saved through faith; and that not of yourselves: it is the gift of God.

- **Acts 2:38** - Repent and be baptized every one of you in the name of Jesus Christ for the remission of sins, and ye shall receive the gift of the Holy Spirit.

There's a song (Oceans, by Hillsong United) that my Aunt Pam often quotes… I'd encourage my readers to Google it as well!

I'm exceptionally fortunate because Pam is so much more than my aunt, which is a position I already hold in high regard. But Aunt Pam is also a dear friend and life-long mentor. She is one of the women I most want to be like. I try to introduce her to as many of my people as possible; she is one of those people you encounter, and you just want to share with the world. The reason is simple, Aunt Pam has lived her life to seek His lead, and to trust His power to perform His miracles. She knows He doesn't need her power; that would be like throwing a gun, versus pulling the trigger. He just needs her obedience. She knows that. And she knows the power of the Almighty is available for her to step into.

By simply observing Aunt Pam over a lifetime, I have learned this:

His power has become part of her identity; therefore, she does not think twice about going 'beyond borders,' or 'walking on water.' And she will do so without fear or apology. She desires to go where He leads because His presence has no boundaries, no limitations, no concerns, and no constraints. The deepest of oceans, He's there! The darkest of valleys, He's there. He will take us to places that we are 100% not capable of handling on our own, but we are 100% prepared and equipped to trust His powerful presence to handle. This allows us to boldly go into the places and spaces He calls us to and leads us to!

Identity within culture teaches us something very different. With a plethora of personality theories to consider, think about this, Freud postulated that we contend with 'id.' His core theory is that our id operates based on the pleasure principle, which demands immediate gratification of needs. The id is one of the three major components of personality Freud considered. I'm not for or against Freudian theories, I just think, like all other human theories, they're simply a human reflection of observing other humans. What I want to point out is that the principle of the id has been glorified throughout human history and modern society isn't any different. It can be seen in the phrase, "Just do it", or "you be you" or "follow your truth." The main problem in that equation is... well frankly, it's that we're human and fallible! We quite literally use the term 'human' when something falls short. We hear a common phrase, "I'm only human." What we are in essence saying is, "I am broken and without perfection; I'm without the knowledge or have within myself the ability to reach perfection."

This brings me back to the discussion about identity, especially regarding the 4R cycle's 4th phase of launching or relaunching into our spheres of influence.

R1, Rest; it's critical to our fragile human bodies to rest, in fact, it's a command, and an act of obedience, not an option. R2, Rejuvenate, we are told to rejuvenate, with fellowship and to count it joy and to enjoy all He has carefully crafted for enjoyment. R3, Revive, the wisdom of the Word is straightforward to plan, to hold a growth mindset, and to gain new tools through discipleship and learning opportunities. These three disciplines allow us to be in a healthy place and space physically, mentally, emotionally, and spiritually so that we can launch, and then relaunch... and then relaunch again into the places and spaces of influence and ministry that Abba has called us into!

Let's make our wellness count!

Think about all the different names used to describe you. Mom, sis, honey, etc. Names, by their nature, come with identity. That's why the Bible is overtly clear to give your kids a good one. Make it count! And when an identity change was needed, we see God change some names... on a few occasions; from Saul to Paul, and one of my favorites is Sarai to Sarah. Not much of a change at first glance, and they both mean Princess. But ultimately, Sarah, the new name, means, a Princess who holds a covenant with God! Ok, we hear you God... that's an identity empowerment for sure! One of my mentors used to tell us that people either live out the potential of their 'name' or manifest the opposite! Interesting to think about.

Tonya means grace, and though I am not known to be a 'graceful' person in movement... these hips don't lie... I am well known to be the recipient of His Great Grace in my life! According to 5 different professionals, at several different points throughout my life, I'm supposed to be dead. There's a throwback scene from the comedy film "Monty Python and the Holy Grail" that always goes through my mind. "Bring out your dead!" is being shouted by a 'body collector' as you see an older man laid out in a wheelbarrow being hauled away. Slowly, the man lifts his head up and says, "I'm not dead yet!" ... if you haven't seen it, it's funny, I promise. It also encapsulates how I sometimes feel. To date, we have survived 6 Cancer diagnoses, 5 organ removals, 4 rounds of Chemo, 3 rounds of radiation, 2 transplants, and everyone sings with me, "And a partridge and a pear tree!" Welcome to my world! And yes, I said 'we' because I couldn't have survived, much less thrived without my amazing husband, family, Church, and multiple tribes of Code Grape girls! And I don't use 'survive' just metaphorically, I also use it literally!

The following are lessons about attempting to relaunch well into my sphere of influence with impact, that I have picked up through the many different names that help form my identity. Some with success, and some with... well, you win some, you learn some! What you will see, is that I surround myself with people phenomenally 'more' or 'better' than me... more intelligent, more capable, more beautiful, more talented, better engaged, more disciplined, wiser, and more obedient. I have been blessed for sure, but I have also been intentional with the people I collect to be in my sphere of influence that can influence me! And to be honest, it's so that I am better equipped to bless and pour into others who are within my sphere of influence to disciple, teach, or empower.

Chick-a-Pea & Big Girl

What a gift to have parents who loved God and trained me while I was young to love God and make Him the central focus and purpose of my life. Shockingly, I was not always the most compliant child...sure, I was loving, but I was cheeky and strong-willed. Honestly, it got to the point where I would just do what I knew was going to get me into trouble and then take my mom the wooden spoon and tell her it was time! True story, but it's funnier when my mama tells it!

I learned from both my parents the importance of 'speaking life' into my children... those that I'm legally responsible for and those that find themselves in my sphere of influence! My precious mama called me Chick-a-Pea or 'Chick' for short. She taught me to love people with my life... I watched her do this my entire life. She has always been the host'ess with the most'est! She is a culinary genius in the kitchen and miraculous with a glue gun! I seriously wanted to make and bedazzle a glue gun holster for her, but never did. You know, it's never too late, maybe that can be this year's Christmas present! My mama, affectionately known as 'Mama Claire' around the world to hundreds if not thousands now is honestly the most creative person I know AND the most radical prayer warrior I know! There's a Charles Spurgeon quote that sums up what I learned from watching and modeling after my mom, "True prayer is neither a mere mental exercise nor a vocal performance. It is far deeper than that, it is a spiritual transaction with the Creator of Heaven and Earth."

My mama taught me to, "Love people with your life" and "change their lives and the atmosphere around them with your intercession!"

My daddy, also known as Papa Lynn, is one of the bravest, strongest men I know and a brilliant 'girl dad.' Even when he didn't know what he was doing, he naturally stepped into the role of protector and 'giver' of identity. I was told early on how beautiful and valuable I was, mind you, let me set a more accurate stage… glasses, braces, awkward long legs, you get the picture… it's funny how I look back at photos from the 70s and 80's and I'm like, "What?! You guys dressed me up like that on purpose? And you even let me go out in public like that?!" Yep, right amid those stages, my daddy made sure I knew I was beautiful; I was capable and I was valued, and no one could ever take that away because I was his, and he said so! The nickname Big Girl came as a result of daddy teaching me that I was competent, or capable of learning when I wasn't. My dad had plenty of anger and other issues he was working out, but that was usually on all the other humans around him. I had the unique perspective of being his little girl and it shaped the way I see the world, my place in it, and that obstacles are only opportunities for me to learn to maneuver around, with, or overcome!

My daddy taught me that my identity has nothing to do with my accomplishments, nor the other people around me. I am beautiful and valuable because he said so. My papa gave me a 'Jesus with skin-on' example to understand that I am who my Heavenly Father says I am… not the mirror, not the culture, and definitely not bullies who may have tried to steal my joy… my identity rests safely in Abba's hands, even when I don't feel it, or deserve it… that's the power of identity and speaking life into those around you!

Sis, Friend, and Ton

I have two amazing brothers, too many Kingdom siblings to count, and a magnificent Code Grape tribe of sisters. Most of them call me 'Sis' or 'Ton.' I have one dearest sister who calls me 'friend,' in fact, when we first met, she would say, "Hey friend" and I remember at first thinking hmm, I don't ever remember someone calling me that, referred to as friends sure, but to call me a friend as a name identity was different for me. The more I have come to be friends with Jesus and understand that relationship with him, the more I LOVE that He calls me friend. Proverbs 17:17 and John 15:13 bring a true honor and understanding to that title!

Wow, He not only loves me, He likes me, He would die for me… in fact, He proved it and He did… and He calls me friend! I want to thank my dear friend Ann for teaching me that and for calling me 'friend!' I know for a fact when I hear that familiar voice, "Hey friend!" my heart swells and my face automatically lights up as I know that's my Annie! And after all these years, travels, and sticky situations, she still calls me friend… and she means it!

Garden Girls

These are my closest and longest friends. The term comes from the "Garden of Gethsemane" a place of great importance to Jesus. It's talked about in all four Gospels as a place where Christ retreated into deep prayer, and a time of agony before His arrest and crucifixion, and near where He ascended to heaven in the Book of Acts. Essentially His 'Swan Song' act. I figure that if Jesus took his most trusted into the Garden, then I better take my most trusted with me when I go into my own situations of 'Gethsemane.' I hope at some point in life you have the privilege of meeting one of the nearest and dearest, named Lisa. If not my Lisa, then perhaps someone 'Lisa'esk.' In addition to being a lead worshiper, lover of nations, and devoted disciple, she also modeled for me 'doing life with others' to bring God glory! When we were in college, I remember watching her come down the stairs with a book and a twinkle in her eye and I asked, "Where are you going?" I thought she was about to go on a date or something with her glowing face... to which she replied, "I'm going to go spend some time with Jesus, be back in a couple of hours!" I had to rethink my entire life and relationship with Jesus at that point! I was pretty sure she loved him more than I did! It just hadn't occurred to me before that, that my relationship with Him could be, should be, one of great personal delight. He had been Savior and Lord for a long time, I knew him in the context of Abba, but friend? I knew He called me friend, but I guess I just glossed over it until then...

Lisa and so many of my Garden Girls have taught me that my relationship with Jesus is real, He's my friend, meaning He's fun and interactive. He's definitely NOT boring, just ask Annie, Kate, or Jessica, any of my travel companions through the years!

Ta Ta or Ta

This is one of my favorite and most endeared names. When my stunning niece Princess was born, she changed all our lives! Cessa couldn't say Tonya, so 'Ta-Ta' is what stuck and carried on to all other nieces and nephews! My oldest brother Damon looks like Santa Claus, so he has always been a big hit with the kids! Not to mention he is fun and funny! My middle brother John is one of the most amazing men that I know. He holds all my respect given what he has survived and has chosen to become for God and his family! He is one of the "Lost Boys" of Sudan and officially became my brother in 2001 after he received refugee status in the US. Check out the resources to learn more about the "Lost Boys." That's an epic story for another time. The short is that I was working for World Relief Refugee Services, and I had the privilege of helping resettle the 72 Lost Boys brought to our area of Fort Worth, TX. My entire family, friend circles, and Church were brought in to help, and everyone rallied to love and serve these amazing heroic young men. My mom and dad became mom and dad to my new 72 Sudanese brothers with a massive birthday celebration on Jan. 1. Refugees that don't know their exact birthday are all given Jan. 1. Since my birthday is Dec. 31, a huge party for all of us only made sense. And for about 10 years or so, it was a staple celebration for our entire community!

John had spent a lot of one-on-one time with my mom and dad and held a special place in their hearts from the beginning. However, when he turned ill, my family jumped into action, and he needed more support than his current status allowed him. So, we adopted him! Every little girl wants a baby brother or sister! I was the youngest, so finally, at the age of 20, I got my brand-new, 'baby brother' who was actually 21! So, he's older and I'm still the youngest! So close! John's addition to our family has been such a sweet gift from God. Over time, John married my amazing sister-in-love Abiar, and a year later we had Princess! She was the most beautiful baby I had ever seen! A couple of years later came AJ. What?! Another perfect baby?! What are the odds of having two gorgeous babies… I mean, let's face it, some babies come out looking a bit like Benjamin Button, but these two children were perfect in every way!! It's amazing how precious and endearing tiny humans become when they are yours! I mean, instantaneously I would have taken a bullet for either one of those amazing kids and that was after seeing them for only seconds. As any parent can attest, it only grows stronger, it's almost indescribable. A dear friend and borrowed-mom, Beth, always said, "It's like watching your heart walk around outside your chest." She nailed it! That's exactly what it's like!

When Princess was three and AJ was one, a set of circumstances led to them being in my care… What an honor! Getting to be a part of raising these two amazing humans has blessed my life beyond words. It also brought tremendous perspective! Princess has taught me resilience in the face of fear. AJ has taught me persistence amid trials.

As their Tata, they have both taught me that the human heart is malleable, with the capacity to grow as large as you will let it!

And being that they're both teenagers in this current stage of life… I have discovered that my daily mantra, "His Grace is Sufficient" has never been truer! Go ahead, change my mind!

Cuz - Cousin Crew

Ok, so this is another near and dear name! Let me explain… as you have discovered, I have brothers. I have many 'cultivated' sisters, but as far as those who have to claim me because we are related, I didn't get to grow up with sisters. I did, however, grow up with my Oklahoma Cousin Crew! If I'm being honest, these three women have impacted my life in such manifold ways that I can probably attribute or blame them – depending on whom you talk to, for why I am the woman I am!

My mom's family was from California, so naturally, she and my Aunt Donna married Marines. That's right, we're all military brats! However, very few Marines were from California, so that meant they married and brought their California brides to their home states. Luckily for me, my dad was from Texas, and luckily for my mama and my mercy-heart Aunt Donna, married my Uncle Jay who is from Oklahoma. This meant that my mom and aunt, who were far away from home, were only a few hours apart from one another. Therefore, the Oklahoma Cousin Crew and the Texas Cousins were together for

EVERY holiday and any moment in between that our moms could make happen!

Punkin, Missy, BabyJ, and I had no idea at the time how important these growing and bonding years would become to us as adults. They truly are the closest thing I have to sisters. In addition to our Pajama Pearls, to be explained later, Punkin even made matching "Cousin Crew" shirts. And yes, we wear those matching T-shirts every time we're all together! No one else understands, but we are SUPER proud we all belong to each other!

Deanna... whom I call Pun'kin, is the oldest. She has always been the coolest, the prettiest, the funniest, and the "smartest!" Pun'kin has the heart to worship and bring God glory with her growth and obedience. She has a God-given gift of 'growing and training' preschoolers. The mug on her desk says, "Goal Today: Keep the Tiny Humans Alive..." I have watched this early childhood specialist develop, grow, and wield big and chaotic personalities from these tiny humans, into brilliant, behaved, and emboldened human beings of integrity! She doesn't just 'keep them alive' she brings them 'to life!' She helps them develop self-control, critical thinking, and foundational baselines for educational and social development. These skills set the tone for the rest of their lives! She helps them grow and make sense of the world around them in very confusing and chaotic times. And if you've ever worked with preschoolers, it's kind of like herding cats! When you find a good preschool teacher, hold on to them for life - they are worth their weight in diamonds and pearls! She teaches them that they were designed by The Creator, on purpose, and for a purpose. It's absolutely amazing to watch her in her element. And now that she's a 'Glammy", watching her with Emma is just as mesmerizing!

Punkin traveled with me to the Middle East a few years ago. I asked her to step out of her comfort zone and teach some of our teachers what she knew about early childhood instruction, Montessori, and classroom environment. She's not used to teaching adults, 'they're a lot bigger' and they 'already critically think!' It took a lot of coaxing and promises of chocolate, but eventually, she relented, and WOW… it was impressive how fantastic she was as a trainer. She brought knowledge and hands-on mentoring like she had been in that role for years and years. Her teacher-students couldn't say enough amazing things about what they were learning from Deanna. As I popped my head in to check on her, I overheard a conversation she had with some teachers' aides and I loved what she said about curiosity:

Anyone can eventually teach any student a lesson or a task if they have enough patience, but if you can show them how to learn by creating and tapping into their curiosity, you have them hooked for life… they will begin to learn independently, and they might even become life-long learners!" – Punkin, a.k.a. Deanna Jackson.

I believe Abba set an innate curiosity in man. And, when we are salt and light, I believe the world is curious and will want to 'taste' and 'see' that the Lord is good!

Missy… Awe, Missy… she's the good one! There's not a single human alive who has met Missy who didn't walk away thinking she was the sweetest. She's the middle-sis with blonde hair and a heart of compassion that's bigger and sweeter than her southern accent! Missy taught me as a child the discipline of Bible Study and Prayer and the fabulous discipline of celebration.

Missy and I were closest in age and the best of friends growing up. We would laugh for hours on end, make up songs, and don't get me started on the family road trips we all took together to California that required us to be in the same car for two days straight! That's probably the reason we're all so close. It was either love each other or kill each other… I think it worked out well as we all survived! Some of our long family road trips can only be described as National Lampoon adventures! Missy and her husband serve in Mongolia, but long before that, Missy's heart has always been for the underdog, the under-seen, and the misunderstood. I've never met someone else who has such an uncanny ability to immediately see the value in others and seek ways to add value to their lives! Missy has taught me so much about perseverance, but more than anything, to be a voice and a resource for 'the least of these.'

Sometimes, the ones who need us the most are the ones who fight it the most! Missy taught me that, "if you are frustrated or annoyed with someone, make them your favorite!" It will change everything! Go ahead, say it won't!

Baby J… And last, but not least is Jessica, who was born a few years after the rest of us. So, when Jessica was born, it was like we had our very own living baby doll!! She was perfect in every way! I think outside of our own children, she was the only other human we ever felt that way about… still do actually! Jessica is such a special and unique person. When I was going to school at OBU, I only lived an hour or so away from their home in Muskogee. De and Missy were grown, but Jess was still at home, and around the age of 12, she would come and stay with me for a week or two at a time. Don't worry, she was homeschooled at that time, and it was more like she had an internship. That's right, my own personal 12-year-old assistant on a college campus! So, her career started young! What really happened is that I had a front-row seat to watch one of the most dedicated disciples I've ever met grow into a brilliant and beautiful disciple-making disciple! I had a heart for missions early on and I didn't know any better than to just include her in everything. And luckily for me, she didn't know any better than to join in! Luckily for both of us, Aunt Donna trusted this crazy college kid to take care of her pre-teen!

Our partnership in international cross-culture missions flourished and has carried into both of our adult lives, personally and professionally. Jessica has traveled to more countries with me than most. I think she has been to over 30 countries with me, maybe more, but I'll let her fact-check the total at a later date. She and her husband currently live and serve overseas full-time with Middle Eastern nations. The sheer volume of stories, laughs, tears, hospitals, and sketchy border-crossings that Jessica and I have encountered together is its own book series! In fact, I'm not even able to put into words all I have gleaned from observing her life dedicated to the King of Kings. There's another quote by Chuck that embodies how Jessica approaches the world and her part in it.

"If sinners be damned, at least let them leap to Hell over our dead bodies. And if they perish, let them perish with our arms wrapped about their knees, imploring them to stay. If Hell must be filled, let it be filled in the teeth of our exertions, and let not one go unwarned and un-prayed for."

~ Charles Spurgeon

In Jessica's language, "Love with every fiber in your being... love like you mean it, even when it seems too much... no matter the cost, go after peoples' hearts and souls... the cost is always worth it!" This is pretty evident in her daily life! And though she may be the youngest, she's one of the wisest people I know!

Doc & Ms.

To my students, K-12, college, post-grad, and adults, I am often referred to as "Doc" or "Ms." I have a soft-spot for my ESL students and love how "Doc" sounds like "Duck" in most accents! Seriously, take an opportunity to teach ESL, the students will change your life! I think one of the greatest lessons I have ever learned as a teacher is that my sphere of influence has the weight to change minds, speak life, and alter trajectories. With that said, the responsibility of that requires me to submit to the Holy Spirit regularly, because I genuinely want any of my students, or those I am discipling, to become World Changers. I want them to know who God says they are! I desperately want them to know their identity in Christ so they too can be disciple-making disciples. They have taught me what happens when I use my sphere of influence well... and when I don't! Father forgive us for our foolishness in our twenties!

Being a teacher has taught me everyone has a sphere of influence. It has also taught me to ask the question, "How will you use the influence God has given you?!" Let me encourage you... Use your forces for good!

Babes

That's right, my husband calls me 'Babes.' Not babe, but babes... I remember laughing the first time I heard him say that and asking, "How many babes are you talking to?" To which he replied, just you Babes, you're more than enough! I wasn't sure if that was sweet endearment or a little jab at me possibly being 'too much!' But in true Tonya fashion, I will take it as a compliment until you tell me directly it wasn't! Say I won't! (That's a shout-out for you Annie!) I have had some pretty extensive medical circumstances, and painful journeys of loss requiring emotional grieving in my time, but the Lord brought Jonathan, aka Fitz, into my life at just the right time. To be honest, when we met, I thought it was 'just the wrong time', but God intervened and preserved one of the greatest gifts to ever come into my life. Fitz is genuinely an amazing husband... don't get me wrong, he's a total engineer nerd who has more dad jokes than a dad-joke book, but he's my amazing nerd! Jonathan has a gift of faith. I have faith and it's real and it's deep, but I have to intentionally work and renew my mind to hold my faith nearby. Fitzi's gift of faith allows him to have, hold, speak, and share with absolute certainty in the God who backs it up! This has been a core component of strength for us. He has been an absolute rock with certainty when all else seemed shaky and uncertain.

When we married, it was later in life, and he married me knowing I had a terminal illness. We have walked through intense medical situations, the loss of loved ones, and the loss of finances due to medical. According to statistics, we hit the three top reasons for divorce! Luckily, Fitz meant it when he said, "In sickness or health!" Upon being told I was terminal, the doctor told Fitz to look at the bottom of my right foot. We both looked at each other and were like, ok, that's unusual, but he's the brilliant oncological hematologist so even though I have a terminal blood cancer illness, sure, "give me that foot!" While trying to examine and follow instructions, Dr. Johnson said, "Do you see it?" Jonathan replied, "I don't really see anything, but I'm not sure what I'm looking for." To which Dr. Johnson replied, "Exactly, you don't see an expiration date at the bottom of her foot. Medicine is just practice, and we can only give you our best understanding of the circumstances. Even though it's our understanding Tonya has 3 months to three years, we don't really know. Even though we recommend you prepare for difficulty and hospice care, nobody really knows how much life and fight are still in her! Modern technology is advancing every day. We will take it one day at a time."

So, after hearing that, I determined, that no matter how much time we do or don't have, we will attempt to serve the Lord and ask Him to show us how to 'die well.' That sounds good, right?! Interestingly enough, all Jonathan heard was "There's no expiration date." He proceeded to read the scripture that spoke about life to dry bones, and all he heard from Dr. Johnson that day, was that we had plenty of life to live! Talk about a different perspective. There is so much more to this story, and we understand that the Father chooses, at different times, to heal in different ways, but I learned that day that I had a 'journey of healing' to go through. I also learned that having a partner with a different perspective on life, though sometimes can be the most frustrating thing about him, has many times become the most amazing and powerful thing about him. Jonathan had to physically take care of me, early on in our marriage, and then again six years later when I was diagnosed with a Stage 4 situation. Talk about love. The man is straight dedicated, and I couldn't image my world without him.

Through it all, our collective takeaway has been this: No matter the circumstance, no matter the trial, no matter the pain, no matter the frustration or disappointment, our God is Great. Our God is able. Our God heals. Our God is sufficient. Our God is peace. And Our God is freedom…

We stand firmly in the promise of Joshua 1:9, so we get to be bold, strong, and courageous without fear or discouragement because the Lord our God, will be with us, every step of the way!

That means, no matter the bondage or circumstance we find ourselves in... God's got us, our Church Tribe's got us, so we've got this!

I appear to have learning amnesia because I tend to need to 'relearn' so many of these lessons regularly... but I truly do want to be obedient and use the tools of wellness available to me through His Word, and launch into my calling, my spheres of influence, with Kingdom impact... Let's do it together... for His glory, our blessings, and the poured-out benefit of blessings and hope of salvation for others!

Let me encourage you... Step into your birthright of the Abrahamic Covenant and watch the world around you, including yourself, be daily redeemed by the King of Transformation!

Well Done Good & Faithful

Spotlights on Organizations & Groups "Doing it well!"

Relaunching is all about being His hands and feet.

We don't need to do more...
we need to make it more about Him.

Healthy Disciples:

- Obey His commands || *Rest*
- Practice His commands || *Rejuvenate*
- Learn His commands || *Revive*
- Then teach & fulfil His commands || *Relaunch*

Then wash, rinse, and repeat! The scripture tells us in Philippians 2:12 that in this life, there is a working out of our salvation... often through fear and trembling, but in this process, we can hold fast to His promises because He is good!

"You cannot stay where you are and go with God. You cannot continue doing things your way and accomplish God's purpose in His ways. Your thinking cannot come close to God's thoughts. For you to do the will of God, you must adjust your life to Him, His purposes, and His ways."

~ Dr. Henry Blackaby

Christ's Haven for Children

~ Cassie McQuitty

Chief Executive Officer
www.christhaven.org

Mission: Christ Haven is centered around the core values of Normalcy, Dignity, and Hope. We are located in the North Fort Worth/Keller, Texas area and provide a trauma-informed, family model of care for displaced children, teens, and young adults.

What a sincere pleasure it was interviewing Cassie. Christ's Haven inspires us as they love at-risk youth and foster children. The ministry embodies the 4R concept by providing a safe place for children and youth to shelter within a family context, receive mentorship and instruction, learn the skills they need for success, and then launch out into independent living. For two years, my family had the opportunity to serve in this sweet ministry as houseparents under her leadership. It was such a unique opportunity to gain experience from Cassie in how to navigate change within the organization as the Lord brought her on as the CEO. Cassie brought such joy and compassion to the campus for both the families serving on staff and the vulnerable youth and children under our care. Her fierce faith and renewed vision for what the Lord is doing in this has been a game changer for the direction the organization is heading in. Cassie, thank you for sharing with us about the mission and heart of the beautiful work God has called you to.

~ Amy

Interview Content with
Cassie McQuitty

How many years have you been in your field? What led you to this field?

I have been in the nonprofit field for more than 20 years. I was led in this direction because I have always wanted to love and serve people. With a degree in psychology, I started my career in a corporate role and was fortunate to be able to change over to the nonprofit sector shortly after.

How has your personal faith impacted your work?

I am a Christian, non-denominational. My faith and love of Jesus impact everything I do in this work. I know that my team and organization are called to be the hands and feet of Jesus when families and children need us most. I also know whole healing only comes from the relationship with Christ. We have the unique opportunity to help the children we serve to focus on spiritual well-being as well as physical and emotional health.

Tell us about your family, and how family plays a role in the work you do.

I have been married to my husband for 20 years and have two daughters ages 11 and 13. My family is my everything. They are my rock, my biggest cheerleaders, the people I am most proud of and work hardest for. My entire family, including extended, are part of the mission at Christ's Haven. They believe in what we are doing here and have willingly made sacrifices so we can serve well.

Tell us about Christ's Haven.

Christ's Haven for Children is a children's home located in Keller, Texas. We are a trauma-informed, family-based model of care focused on normalcy, dignity, and hope for the children we serve. We serve displaced youth ages 18-24 when their families cannot otherwise care for them. On our 50+ acre campus, we have a neighborhood of homes where we employ one houseparent who lives on campus with the spouse, and we place up to eight children in their home. Additionally, we serve young adults ages 18-24 in our Supervised Independent Living program, where they can pursue secondary education, work full-time, or do a combination of both while receiving case management, counseling, and curriculum to continue to prepare them for the next season of life. Finally, we recently began our Family Resource Center, where we serve foster families, families at risk of needing placement, young adults who have aged out of foster care, and recently reunified families. These families receive weekly meal boxes, free crisis counseling, parent, and caregiver education and case management. This newest program allows us to help in the prevention of poverty-related neglect.

When it comes to wellness, how has your organization stewarded the concept of the 4Rs?

I think the thing I am most proud of as the leader of Christ's Haven is the Relaunch emphasis we employ in our programs and how we serve families. Being a 70-year-old organization, we have to intentionally self-reflect, continue to learn, and be willing to be nimble in how we reach and serve our families. Under my leadership, we relaunched and redefined what a family-based model of care looks like. We intentionally serve and pursue our families with the love of a parent making decisions that are individualized for each case. This makes our work more difficult and time-consuming but has better long-term outcomes.

How do you implement the 4 R's into your daily life?

When I am away from work, you will find me spending quality time with my family and watching my girls follow their passions in cheer and dance. I am very involved at our church, Milestone, where I serve at Elevate weekly and in other small group environments.

If there was one area that you would desire to implement more of, which would it be?

I could implement more Rest in my daily life. Running a large 24/7 organization and keeping up the busy schedule of our family does not allow for much downtime and when we do have it, I tend to fill up that space as well.

TransformUs Movement Inc

~ Dominique Jones

Co-Founder & Executive Director
www.transformusmovement.com

Mission: TransformUs Movement works to transform underserved communities, one person at a time. From music concerts to humanitarian aid projects, we've mobilized over 60 organizations to work collaboratively, providing tangible needs and empowerment to over 7,800 people across the Dallas-Fort Worth Metroplex.

TransformUs is an exciting ministry in the DFW area that has impacted the lives of thousands of people over the last ten years. We love their emphasis on building relationships to create lasting results among marginalized communities based on values of authenticity, integrity, creativity, diversity, unity, and excellence.

We were excited to interview Dominique Jones to hear more about TransformUs and how the 4Rs play into their ministry. Dominique is deeply committed to empowering others to use their unique talents and abilities to bring lasting transformation to their communities and generations to come, including her own children. We love how she emphasized making them a part of the ministry rather than feeling like the ministry takes away from them. More on that to come...

~ Kate Jordan

Interview Content with
Dominique Jones

Tell us a little about your background and what led you to the work you do.

I've worked in the nonprofit space for over 10 years. While studying global missions and Christian Leadership at CFNI, God birthed a vision in our hearts that we began to develop. Ironically, I have enough credits to have a degree but do not have a degree, which is a reminder that achieving success and walking out of my calling will be by the grace and favor of God (not my credentials)!

I went to college before coming to Christ and was headed down a career path that the Lord had not ordained or called me to long-term. Most of what I have learned, the Holy Spirit taught me "in the trenches" or trials of life and leadership. I'm constantly amazed at the opportunities He has entrusted to me without formal training, yet the results always reveal that the wisdom and revelation of God are undeniable. "My strength is made perfect by your weakness." Nonetheless, I do value continuing education. I received an advanced certificate in Global Missions & Christian Leadership. I've also gotten certified as a nonprofit manager through the CNM Nonprofit Management Certificate program. I am also a licensed real estate agent and am committed to helping the people we serve through our programs find ways to build wealth despite their backgrounds.

How has your faith impacted the work that you do?

I am a Christian, but I do not associate with any denominations (although I have collaborated with and served the vision of various denominations over the years). I am committed to living my life as a devoted Christ follower, fulfilling the Great Commission and equipping believers to walk in their gifts and calling to advance the Kingdom of God.

Tell us about your family, and how your family plays a role in the work you do, directly or indirectly.

I have been married for 15 years and have 3 beautiful children: 14, 8, and 6. My husband and I are co-laborers and partners in ministry and kingdom business. I consider him the visionary behind the TransformUs Movement and the visionary leader. I feel like I "gave birth" to it and have helped to execute and mobilize a team to carry it out and develop the infrastructure to expand our reach and impact.

We have intentionally included our children as we walk in obedience and carry out the work; they have observed the kingdom work since they were babies and now, that they are older, we invite them to serve alongside us as much as they would like. However, we are intentional about avoiding burnout or becoming desensitized or disillusioned by ministry.

Our kids feel a part of the work instead of feeling neglected by the work. In the past, they've helped us feed the homeless in Tent City and package meals for international projects, even if it meant me carrying them in a baby wrap. They've joined us at a women's shelter, playing with the kids. Now that they are older, they are more hands-on behind the scenes as prayer warriors, ideators, camera operators, and even social media managers.

Tell us more about TransformUs.

Since 2013, TransformUs Movement has been building bridges to bring unity, diversity, and transformation to underserved communities. To make a lasting impact, we launched a mentorship program in 2018 to make healthy, empowering relationships and resources more accessible to at-risk young adults. Our mission is to help young adults (ages 18-35) discover and live out their purpose. We offer group mentoring, one-on-one mentoring, life skills training, counseling, and other needed services.

In 2013, my husband Brock and I, and a small team, began hosting local outreach, providing food, clothes, disaster relief and other services. On December 21, 2015, the TransformUs Movement was incorporated, solidifying the vision to transform communities one person at a time. From music concerts to humanitarian aid projects, TransformUs has hosted over 75 collaborative events and empowered more than 8,000 people across the DFW Metroplex and 7 different countries. To make a lasting impact, TransformUs launched a mentorship program for young adults in 2019, to empower young adults to discover and live out their purpose while partnering with us to promote unity, diversity, and transformation in underserved communities.

When it comes to wellness, how has your organization stewarded the different stages?

We have had to implement the relaunch concept a few times over the years. During the lifecycle of a nonprofit, there are inevitably times when you have to adapt, pivot, and revamp to stay relevant. Although our mission has remained the same, our methods have changed quite a bit in various seasons to meet current needs in the community. For instance, in 2017 and 2018, we had an initiative focused on addressing food insecurity. We worked really hard to launch the program and were even awarded funding, but due to circumstances beyond our control, we were unable to launch. We pivoted the next year, recognizing a great need for mentorship. Since then, we have rebranded to better communicate with and reach our target audience. We've refined and clarified our processes and partnerships so we can become more effective. Soon, we will be relaunching differently through a collaborative effort, reaching considerably more young adults.

How do you implement the 4 R's into your daily life?

I love Sunday naps, trying new foods, traveling, dancing, skating, and spending time with my family. I haven't always been the best at the first three, but after losing my mom, I have a renewed commitment to taking care of myself through rest, creating more margin in my schedule, and doing recreational things that are life-giving to me. Our family day is on Friday. We spend intentional time together, having fun and making new memories. Quarterly, I evaluate the goals that I set on an annual basis and make sure that I am staying aligned, or I pivot as needed. Adapting to seasonal changes in life helps me to "relaunch" and stay relevant and true to myself.

Which of the 4Rs needs a bit of work in your life?

I can always use more rest. As a high-capacity leader who is multi-passionate, it's so easy to take on more and more and feel a sense of purpose for it all. I'm learning to create more margins to allow for the unexpected things that life can bring. It also just gives room for breath, being fully present, and adding fun. I'm learning that rest is multidimensional and can look different for every person. As I continue to learn about myself- flaws and all- I'm leaning more into the Lord's rest while working and not working. I want it to be a lifestyle. I don't want to look busy or frazzled. People always comment on the peace they feel, but in this season, I am aiming at my own enjoyment and people seeing a slower, less busy pace.

Bless Your Heart

Faux Pas' and embarrassing or tactless acts or remarks in the crazy social situations we find ourselves!

// You Look So Good //

|| By Shari Walker ||

"You look so good." ... seems to be a common thing people say to someone who is dealing with any kind of diagnosis. Someone asks how things are going, you give a quick update, and sure enough, "Well, you look good." comes out of their mouth.

I don't know, maybe it's just me, but it makes me think I should have an arm or something growing out of my forehead!

// I Thought You Were Dead?! //

|| By Tonya Lincoln ||

Two years after being diagnosed with a terminal illness and taking an early retirement from my job with the local school district, my body dared to get better! I happened to run into a former colleague in downtown Fort Worth while out with my family. We both did a double take and smiled, then started walking toward each other. We reached out to hug each other and the first thing out of his mouth was, "Doc! I thought you were dead?!" To which I simply responded, "If it makes you feel any better, I was supposed to be!" We both laughed. And in all fairness, at that time, I was hearing that same sentiment 2 - 3 times a week!

I love humans, we are so weird! Even Jonathan started saying things like, "I know right? She's like a cat with 9 lives!" He knows how I feel about cats (she says with a disapproving smirk on her face!)

// Mom Mishaps //

|| By Emily Bryant ||

"Anxiety meds for the anti-anxiety yoga instructor to teach the anti-anxiety class. Sounds about right!"

I had reached a true milestone. My youngest was about to start Kindergarten. I was about to have ALL my children in school Monday through Friday. Though I was sad that her preschool years were over, I was excited about the newfound freedom around the corner. What was I going to do with all this time?! I knew exactly what I wanted to do. I wanted to teach yoga, and I wanted to teach at the studio where I had been practicing. Over the past 3-4 years, I had managed to weasel in a class or 2 a week and had fallen in love with hot power yoga. I found it to be incredibly grounding and refreshing, and knew it was a great way for me to steward my body- cardiovascular work, strength, and flexibility were all benefits to this practice, and if I had minimal time, this practice would cover it all in just an hour.

I loved it so much that I had even signed up for a teaching certification the previous fall. All I had to do was finish up a few classes and audition to teach at the studio.

I wanted to influence those around me. I wanted to show them that they too could reach a place of lower anxiety, more confidence, and an increased self-love through this practice. I finally finished the required coursework and class fulfillment for the certification. HOORAY! I was so thankful to my family for making this possible.

I was now certified and could apply at any yoga studio to teach, but I didn't want to apply to just any studio. I wanted to apply at MY studio, the one I had grown to love and appreciate. The requirements were strict, but I auditioned. I just knew I had nailed it, with a minor hiccup or two possibly.

To my disappointment, I did not make it. I knew that I was close, so I set my pride aside and scheduled a second audition for a couple of weeks later. Pushing the nerves aside, I made it through! I had done it. I was going to teach what I loved at the studio that I loved with this new pocket of time that I had without my kids.

The day came to teach my first class. Though I am a certified teacher and have taught children in a classroom setting, this was different. These were adults! Their spinal cords were attached to their brain stems, they had and used critical thinking, and I knew they had high expectations. I thought I was going to throw up. I had to take an anti-anxiety pill to calm down so that I wouldn't forget my sequence, cues, and other important aspects of the class. I was taking a pill to treat the anxiety I was having so that I could in turn teach others to have less anxiety. This was RIDICULOUS. Why did I sign up for this again? It was not supposed to feel this uncomfortable. What was I supposed to do?

When we encounter anxiety in the relaunch phase, it reminds us of our dependence on the Father and often requires us to remember and use the cycle of the 4Rs, Relaunching doesn't mean we've 'arrived!' it means we are in the process of working things out and in the process of applying rest, rejuvenate, and revive to apply these things in the relaunch. Think of it like taking care of our hair: Wash, Rinse, Dry, Style, Repeat! There are times when we have to go back through a cycle sooner than others! And take heart, when we launch or relaunch into our sphere of influence, and it doesn't go as we had planned, there's always hope and joy in remembering that we have a cycle we can plug right back into! Reset with rest, count it joy in the rejuvenation, revive with a new tool to help us succeed, then relaunch again and watch to see how God will get glory!

As for teaching grown humans, I told myself that I would keep walking through the 4R cycle and give it the semester in hopes that the angst would subside.

I am still currently in that semester and working towards the goal! You can pray for me as sometimes the resistance and dread are higher than others. With each class I teach, I am slowly becoming more confident in my ability. I am excited to watch this story unfold- even as ridiculous as it seems at times. Seriously, an anti-anxiety yoga instructor on anxiety pills to help her teach the anti-anxiety class, ha! That sounds about right! And should you want to join, feel free any time! I hear the studio down the street is taking in new clients!

// It's True. I Heard it Once! //

|| By Ann Sullivan ||

I'm Thinking Gilligan's Island Might be a True Story – The 12-Hour Tour!

My husband, Bill, and I had the blessing of living in St Croix, US Virgin Islands early on in our marriage. Before moving to the Caribbean Island, we lived in the Dallas Fort Worth area and decided to take Kiel-boat sailing lessons on Lake Grapevine. We were truly inspired by the nautical lifestyle when we were surrounded by the beautiful clear blue water of the Caribbean Sea. Dear friends of ours from our church offered to gift us a 15-foot Hobie Cat sailboat that previously had belonged to their sons who no longer lived on the island. We spent weeks cleaning up the catamaran, replacing parts and getting it seaworthy.

My husband wanted nothing more than to take me out on the boat. We spoke to our friends the day before we set sail. They provided us with sage advice that included purchasing life jackets and always…. always make sure you have this red rope in hand in case the boat "turtles" (aka turns upside down) so you can right the ship. My husband persistently asked if we should buy a mast float to prevent the boat from turning upside down or being submerged in the water and his question was met with a resounding "no". The day that my husband wanted to test the sails was the day that I was planning to study and prepare for my PA board exam. My husband was very persistent and convinced me to "take a break" to RELAX and enjoy sailing "for a few hours". I should have listened to the gentle promptings of the Lord that said "Don't do it" as we had issues just with setting up the sailboat on dry land. However, we persevered and powered through the difficulties and launched the boat into the water at Cane Bay. The wind immediately caught the sails, and we were being whisked away due north away from the island.

Bill was caught by surprise when the catamaran took off like a shot and was dragging him behind the boat through the waves. I was unfortunately the one in control of steering the rudder. Mind you, I was taught how to steer a boat with a keel, not without. They do not operate the same. The next few minutes were a blur. I moved my hand ever so slightly and that catamaran turned on a dime and immediately turtled. Bill and I tried everything to right the boat including using the infamous "red rope". The boat took on water immediately in the two hulls and wouldn't budge. I do remember vividly, the tall blue and red sail looked beautiful flowing in the water below our feet. Bill decided to stay with the boat as I decided to swim to shore for help.

As I made it close to shore, I stood on a rock to survey the landscape. The water line was covered in black spiney sea urchins. As I stood on the rock and watched as the tide went out. I spotted a narrow area the width of a balance beam that was void of the scary sea urchins. I took off my life preserver and wrapped it around one fist in case I needed it for balance. In that moment, I praised God for preparing me for a moment like this with all my years of practice as a competitive gymnast. The area where we were sailing was sparsely populated. So, you can imagine my surprise that once I landed on shore, a man was standing there asking me if I needed assistance. He helped me up the berm to his vehicle on the street above. Driving the vehicle was a former patient of mine from the hospital here to rescue me. They drove me back to the beach bar where others had congregated to watch our fiasco unfold in the bay. Ultimately, a dive crew from a nearby shop attempted to rescue Bill with their inflatable Zodiac boat but was unsuccessful. After several hours, we resigned to calling our friends and asking for help. Our Hobie Cat was so waterlogged that even a large boat with multiple engines was unable to right it.

Eventually, we used that powerful boat to drag it to shore. We utilized 8 strong men to use their brute strength to turn the boat over to allow the hulls to drain. As if this wasn't enough, we were a glutton for punishment. While we were attempting to turn the boat over, the only set of keys for our jeep on the island got accidentally knocked out of my pocket and into the ocean to never be seen again. This was the moment my husband finally started to lose his cool but only momentarily as I began to cry. He had promised me a relaxing 3-hour tour which turned into a 12-hour ordeal.

We honestly praise Jesus that we are alive to share this now humorous tale and share the wisdom we have gleaned from the experience. Also, if I'm counting blessings, this ultimately made our marriage stronger, and we still laugh whenever we recount this tale.

God's Got You
We'll Walk with You
You've Got This!

<u>Practical Applications</u>

Tools, devotions, journals, and prayers to help you tap into your privilege as a child of God, use your gorgeous guidebook, the Bible, step into your trusted Code Grape Tribe, and experience Extraordinary Wellness in your everyday!

|| By: Natalyia Rutherford & Ann Sullivan ||

In Merriam-Webster dictionary, relaunch means to restart, reintroduce, propel forward, put into operation or motion again.

- Have you ever failed at something?
- Have you ever felt stagnant in life or your walk with Christ?
- Have you ever felt like your relationships are backsliding?

Well, you are NOT alone!
As my girl, **Taylor Swift** says, *"Shake it off"*.

I believe the Lord allows us to go through these moments of failure, stagnation, or backsliding only to propel us further than we could ever imagine.

I grew up in the Midwest and hadn't traveled outside of the area until I was in college. My best friends from PA school would tell me of their incredible dreams of being missionaries in foreign countries. I had NO such dreams or aspirations. However, the Lord changed all of that after He sent me on my first mission trip to Thailand to work in a refugee camp after the tsunami in 2005. He ignited inside of me a love for humanity that would only continue to grow with compounding interest and that no one could snuff out.

When I tell others my testimony about the love of Christ and how He exceeded my own expectations for my own life, I often cling to this scripture:

"Now to Him who is able to do immeasurably more than we ask or imagine, according to His power that is at work within us."

~ Ephesians 3:20

We all have moments where we are consumed with or distracted by life, where our relationship with Christ can flow, and sometimes struggle, questioning everything if we're being honest.

We all know it is easy to dwell on our past mistakes, missteps, and failures. Satan loves it when we ruminate on such things because it takes our focus off the ONE who matters most, Jesus. The Lord makes it very clear in the bible in Isaiah 43:18-19, "Forget the former things; do not dwell on the past. See, I am doing a new thing! Now it springs up; do you not perceive it? I am making a way in the wilderness and streams in the wasteland."

We love this scripture as it's a beautiful depiction that the Lord tells us NOT to dwell on our past but to actually forget it. This scripture also shows us that He can do something unimaginable such as provide a flowing stream of water in a dry and barren desert.

Despite our humanness and MANY imperfections, He continues to surprise us by allowing us to do things in our lives that we never imagined. He is always propelling us forward while He is continually ready to renew us and relaunch us past our original starting point.

Rethinking my ReLaunch

"Then I heard the voice of the Lord saying, 'Who shall I send and who will go for us?' And I said, 'Here I am; send me!'"

~ Isaiah 6:8-13

Where do you think the Lord is relaunching you after attaining your newfound rest, rejuvenation, knowledge, and skill sets?

____

____

____

____

____

____

____

"Commit to the Lord whatever you do, and he will establish your plans."

~ Proverbs 16:3

Write a prayer asking the Lord to confirm your steps and intervene if it is not in line with HIS will & Kingdom plans.

____

____

Life Giving | How is the Lord asking you to use your talents to be a blessing to others?

"There is one body, but it has many parts. But all its many parts make up one body. It is the same with Christ. We were all baptized by one Holy Spirit. And so, we are formed into one body. It didn't matter whether we were Jews or Gentiles, slaves or free people. We were all given the same Spirit to drink. So, the body is not made up of just one part. It has many parts."

~ 1 Corinthians 12:12- 14

Each part of the body has a different form and function, but each is valuable and essential to the body of Christ.

Since everyone gives and receives information differently as the body of Christ, what is an example of "life-giving" to you?

____
____
____
____
____
____

What blessings or talents do you possess that could be "life-giving" to others?

____
____
____
____
____
____

Accountability | Are you more concerned with pleasing people and keeping up a façade? Or are you truly vulnerable and transparent with your accountability partners?

____
____
____
____
____
____

Do you ask for accountability in walking through your Extraordinary Wellness goals?

____

____

____

____

____

____

Do you have someone to encourage you to prioritize, normalize the 4Rs, and set healthy boundaries?

____

____

____

____

____

____

Use My Tools | Which of the tools (i.e.: internal, visible, adjustment, language) listed in the "Revive" chapter would you like to master? Give an example or scenario of when you might utilize this tool.

____

____

____

____

____

____

Navigation | Sometimes we don't recognize our own "indicator flags". However, we can discern "indicator flags" in those closest to us. Are you open to receiving feedback when family, friends, or those in our sphere of influence alert us to warning signs?

____
____
____
____
____
____

Connection | How will you set aside time to connect with your Tribe (daily, weekly, monthly, bimonthly)? You should define what this looks like with your tribe as people have different love languages, ideas regarding: connection, and what quality time looks like.

____
____
____
____
____
____

Have a 4R Plan

Think through your current routines and rituals. What routines or rituals need to be added, updated, or eliminated that might otherwise hinder your relaunch?

(Take a moment to look back and review what you wrote at the beginning of the Relaunch Culture section.)

PRAYER OF RELAUNCHING

Dear Heavenly Father,

Thank you for knowing us intimately and loving us despite our imperfections! There is nothing that we can say or do that is hidden from you. I thank you for my weaknesses and failures because this is when I can see you performing your greatest miracles.

Lord, I surrender my life, all that it is, and all that it can be. I cast all my anxiety and fear to you. Lord, renew my spirit and allow my heart to sing a new song.

Thank you for being a God of details. I wait expectantly upon you, Jesus, for my next steps no matter how big or small they may be. My hope is in you, Lord!

Amen.

Chapter Six

Thank You, Readers. . .

Thank you for allowing our Code Grape Tribe to share with you the stories of the amazing women who help step into God's Word and use the tools He has given us to experience Extraordinary Wellness along the way.

Thank you for allowing us to join you on a small part of your journey through Extraordinary Wellness!

We want to leave you with this!

We believe we have the coolest and most important calling in the world:

- We are called to be silent before him and rest.
- We are called to count it all joy and lean in!

- We are called to step into his strength and truth and to learn healthy tools.

So that,

- We can step towards the calling of our lives to join Him in His work. We can go boldly into the sphere of influence He has called us to!

You were born for such a time as this!

HE KEEPS ALL OF HIS PROMISES

And remember... When people say **where is God?** It's not an indictment on Him, it's an indictment on the Church. Let's be more like the Creator, of whose image we were created!

- God commanded rest, Jesus rested, and we must rest.
- God commanded rejuvenation, Jesus had joy, and we must have joy.
- God commanded revival, Jesus revived, and we must revive.
- God commanded relaunching, Jesus relaunched, we must relaunch.

Christ doesn't sacrifice others to save self,

He always sacrifices himself for others.

Let's do this!

About the Authors & Contributors

Tonya Chancey Lincoln is a redeemed, daughter of God the Creator with a desire to join Christ in His work. Tonya and her husband Jonathan (Fitz), live in North Texas and work throughout the Middle East, Asia, and Africa. She beams when she talks about Princess and AJ. She and Fitz take great pride in the abundant family and friend tribes around the globe they have cultivated together! They love all things multi-cultural.

Tonya is an international speaker, vision-caster, trainer, and writer. She has served the ministry of Hope Farm in Texas, since 2019. For fun, she authors and designs curriculum and program frameworks for non-profits, schools, and training companies globally. She is a highly trained educational and behavioral specialist, with a unique niche as an international diplomat and anti-terrorism conflict resolution specialist. Her degrees are in education, leadership, psychotherapy, neurobiology, and diplomacy. She is a cancer and transplant survivor, six times over. She is forever thankful for her amazing team at HANDS Int'l, HANDS Int'l UK, OPAL, Christmas Tree Ranch, Wonder Warriors, and the UN MAWE Project. She has served as a director and advisor on the board for educational and non-profit organizations around the world.

Aimee Rhodes is a wife, a dog mom, the world's best aunt and so many other roles. Aimee is an entrepreneur, counselor, and co-owner of her private practice Transform and Renew PLLC in San Antonio, TX. She holds a doctoral degree in Global Training and development and looks forward to utilizing that knowledge to further the kingdom of God by blending her expertise in mental health, education, and business. She works as a counselor in private practice serving those who have been impacted by childhood and relationship trauma. She lives life with an autoimmune disorder and knows the impact of trauma on human existence. She knows a thing or two because she has seen a thing or two. When she isn't working, she attempts to maintain some balance with friendships, getting in nature, and finding humor in the small things.

Emily Bryant is married to James Bryant and is a mom of 4 kids ages 15, 12, 9, and 6. She has a master's degree in Kinesiology from Texas Christian University. She taught preschool-aged children in a special and general education blend format in Arlington ISD for 5 years. For now, she is a full-time mom. She tries to find humor through all the ups and downs of parenting and enjoys meditating to grow in her faith and relationship with God. She finds the most precious moments to be found when she is still. She teaches yoga at a local studio, volunteers for the PTA at the younger kids' elementary school, and enjoys teaching kids' yoga once a month in a local, underprivileged school. She and her family also host a small group for their local church. She strives for authenticity in herself and her parenting and hopes that her love for God will flow out into her community and loved ones.

Kate Jordan is a traveler, mentor, gardener, and mom to three grown adults, each of whom has chosen a mate and expanded the family. Kate has worked in just about all sides of the nonprofit sector, from ministries to churches, to universities, and from starting small nonprofits to overseeing multiple organizations simultaneously. She recently accepted a position working for a philanthropic foundation and is learning what it's like to be on the grant maker rather than grant seeker side and is loving the opportunity to be a

part of funding some amazing work across the country and around the world. Travel is Kate's particular joy, and she has visited over forty-five countries. Whether the journey is for work, ministry, or pleasure, she loves experiencing new cultures and people groups. Some of the titles Kate has worn through the years are military wife, cross-cultural trainer, team leader, mentor, study abroad coordinator, administrator, executive pastor, missionary, Bible study leader, and most importantly daughter of the most high God and seeker of His face. Currently single and an empty nester, Kate lives in Fort Worth, Texas with her two little French bulldogs, Star and Luna.

Natalyia Rutherford is blessed by her Father, is married to her best friend, and is "mom"/"bruh"/ chauffeur/chef to her two awesome children. Laughing is her favorite. She has a degree from Oklahoma State University in Human Development and Family Science with an emphasis in Child and Family Services. She has worked for ChristianWorks for over ten years collectively (with a few years break to have kids) and considers it an honor to work for an organization that she believes in with her whole heart. When she's not working or running kids around, you'll find her outside getting vitamin D therapy or inside crafting or reading. She's learned that her greatest testimony hasn't been from one or two life-changing events, but that God reveals himself in the everyday - in the mundane, ordinary tasks that fill our days. When we recognize He's there in those moments, we never doubt He'll be there for the big ones. He is good, all the time.

Ann Sullivan is a wife, sister, aunt, daughter, and friend but most importantly a child of God. She grew up in Illinois and Indiana where her family still resides. She has had the privilege of working all over the world as a Physician Assistant in multiple specialties during the last 20+ years. Her passion is serving others, especially in medical/surgical missions. She has been honored to work across the globe alongside several world-renowned non-profit organizations. She and Bill, the love of her life, have been married for just over 15 years. Ann says she is thankful that Bill is super intelligent and so flexible, it has turned out to be an important combination when partnering in ministry as they enjoy the journey God has brought them on. One of her greatest joys is the title of "aunt" to her 16 nieces and nephews. When she's not traveling for missions or to see family and friends, she enjoys daily life in the Florida sun and picking up new hobbies such as languages, guitar, and piano.

Amy Isom was born and raised in Dallas, TX to immigrant parents from Nigeria. Amy surrendered her life to Christ and has not looked back since. She has several degrees in Bible, social work, and counseling. She's a life coach who loves working with couples, families, and trauma work.

She is passionate about soul health and is a joyful wife of 9 years and mother of 1 son. Amy loves laughter and people, is a hugger at heart, a vintage shopper, and an outdoors lover.

Shari Walker has been the Communications Director for Alsbury Baptist Church in Burleson, Texas for the last ten years. Before that, she was a children's minister and pre-teen / youth camp organizer. She has served professionally in ministry for over thirty years. Her passion is video arts and helping people tell their stories through video. She has also worked on national and global campaigns for 5 Star Conference and Expo and See You at the Pole™.

Shari is the wife of a graphic designer and marketing consultant and the mother of two young adults. She received her

Bachelor of Science in Sociology from Howard Payne University. She is a Texas native and resides in Burleson with her husband.

"May the Lord bless you and keep you, May His face shine upon you, and be gracious to you; the Lord lift His countenance upon you and give you peace!"

~ Numbers 6:24-26

Wellness, Now What?!

Resources:

www.CODEGrape.org We are in no way endorsing or have been endorsed by any of the following resources. All of the listed resources can be found online or in other public domains. These are listed without the owner's endorsement of this book or its contents.

QR Code	Name / Website	Key Words
24-7 Prayer	24-7 Prayer www.24-7prayer.com	Website Prayer
Lectio Course 365	Lectio 365 "Learn to meditate on the Bible"	Phone App Prayer Rest
Inner Room	Inner Room "Pray for the people in your sphere of influence."	Phone App Prayer Relaunch

Lectio for Families	Lectio for Families "Go deeper in prayer as a family"	iPhone App Prayer Revive
Who Switched Off my Brain:	Who Switched Off my Brain: Controlling Toxic Thoughts" by Caroline Leaf	Book Revive
Neurocycle App:	Neurocycle App: Manage Stress, Anxiety, & Depression "Rewire & Detox your Brain" By Dr. Leaf	Phone App Thoughts Revive Manage Stress
Christian Works	Christian Works Building healthy homes and families. https://www.christian-works.org/	Website Counseling Rest Revive Relaunch
When Helping Hurts	When Helping Hurts By Corbett & Fikkert	Book Revive Relaunch Missions

Atomic Habits	Atomic Habits By James Clear	Book Revive Relaunch Habits
Tender Care	Tender Care By Wilson & Kronbauch	Book Rest Revive Relaunch Global Workers
What Happens When Women Pray	What Happens When Women Pray By E Christenson	Book Prayer Rest Revive Relaunch
The Celebration of Discipline	The Celebration of Discipline By Richard Foster	Book Rest Rejuvenate Revive Relaunch Celebration Discipline
Men are Like Waffles - Women are Like Spaghetti	Men are Like Waffles - Women are Like Spaghetti By Bill and Pam Farrel	Devotional Study Guide Revive Relaunch Relationships Communication

Men are from Mars, Women are from Venus	Men are from Mars, Women are from Venus By John Gray	Book Guide Revive Relaunch Relationships Communication
The Lost Boys of Sudan	The Lost Boys of Sudan By Mark Bixler	Book Lost Boys Revive Relaunch Trauma Sudan
The Good Lie	The Good Lie Produced by	Movie Lost Boys Revive Relaunch Trauma Sudan
Boundaries	Boundaries: When to Say Yes, How to Say No To Take Control of Your Life By H. Cloud & J. Townsend	Book Rest Revive Relaunch Relationships Communication
Experiencing God	Experiencing God By Henry Blackaby	Book, Bible Study Rest Revive Relaunch Relationships Communication

Faithful to Christ:	Faithful to Christ: A Challenge to Truly Live for Christ By Charles Spurgeon	Book, Bible Study Rest Revive Relaunch Relationships Ministry
The Road Back to You: Enneagram	The Road Back to You: An Enneagram Journey to Self-Discovery By I. Morgan Cron, S. Stabile	Book, Study Rest Rejuvenate Revive Relaunch Relationships Self-Discovery
The Path Between Us: Enneagram	The Path Between Us: An Enneagram Journey to Healthy Relationships By I. Morgan Cron, S. Stabile	Book, Study Rest Rejuvenate Revive Relaunch Relationships Communication
The 5 Love Languages	The 5 Love Languages: The Secret to Love that Lasts By Gary Chapman	Book, Study Love Rejuvenate Revive Relaunch Relationships Communication

Cat & Dog Theology	Cat & Dog Theology: Rethinking Our Relationship with our Master By Bob Sjogren	Book, Study Faith Rest Rejuvenate Revive Relaunch Relationships Communication
Lioness Arising	Lioness Arising: Wake Up and Change Your World By Lisa Bevere	Book Rejuvenate Revive Relaunch Relationships Ministry
Love Does	Love Does: Discover a Secretly Incredible Life in an Ordinary World By Bob Goff	Book Rejuvenate Revive Relaunch Relationships Ministry
Saving Your Marriage Before it Starts	Saving Your Marriage Before it Starts By Les & Leslie Parrott	Book, Test, Study Rest Rejuvenate Revive Relaunch Relationships Marriage

Covered Glory	Covered Glory By Audrey Frank	Book Honor, Shame Relaunch Relationships Muslim Missions
There's a Sheep in My Bathtub	There's a Sheep in My Bathtub: Birth of a Mongolian Church Planting Movement By Brian Hogan	Book Rejuvenate Revive Relaunch Relationships Mongolia Missions
Shadow of the Almighty	Shadow of the Almighty - (Lives of Faith) by Elisabeth Elliot	Book Rejuvenate Revive Relaunch Relationships Ecuador Missions
She Reads Truth	She Reads Truth https://shereadstruth.com/?shem=iosie	App & Podcast Bible studies that are in depth. And discussions via podcast. Can order their hard copy Bible studies as well. Good for reviving.
Mother's Day out programs in local churches for busy moms who need a break or just a shower without a kid attached. Kids can socialize in a safe place.		

Bible Study Fellowship	Bible study fellowship international	Local Bible Studies Connect with fellow believers, women's groups, young adult groups, some even have childcare.
TBRI	TBRI: Trust Based Relational Intervention Training	Training Course Trauma-Informed Training @ The Karen Purvis Institute
Perspectives.org	www.perspectives.org Perspectives.org Mobilizing God's People for God's Global Purpose	Website Perspectives is an awe-inspiring comprehensive study course that is rooted in the Scriptures. It's a multi-faceted learning experience that has profoundly impacted over 250,000 alumni.
YWAM Prayer Journal	Prayer Journal Join a powerful prayer chain around the globe! *Thousands of Christians worldwide use the Planner to organize, journal their prayer times and Bible reading, and systematically pray for the nations - all in one easy-to-use format.*	

Resource Conclusion

Our greatest resource is God the Creator and His spoken Word, the Bible. We will assume that if you read this book, then you are a CodeGrape sister who has made, or is interested in making, a commitment to be a student of Christ. This means He has been made Lord of your life, and you have chosen to take the time needed to be obedient and present with palms up, ready to receive all He has promised to teach and pour into you. Now's the time, if you wait for the time to come, it will always evade you. Make the call, the text, the visit... Get together with your sisters and walk with each other through the fullness of Extraordinary Wellness.

1. **REST |** When we choose to walk in true rest, we find space and grace to breathe... in His presence, chaos and confusion are simply obliterated allowing us a quietness that leads to genuine peace.

2. **REJUVENATE |** Spending regular and adequate time in this state is the catalyst allowing us to soak in, choose, and participate in joy. Not simply settling for the unhealthy practice of always needing to be entertained. This space creates a deep sense of satisfaction with gratitude. Choosing joy from a rested mind is what allows us to be refreshed, and free from the chaos, ready to step into growth.

3. **REVIVE |** In this reviving growth mindset, we experience and see many amazing things:

   a. There will be a real conviction of sin, that leads to repentance. Confronted by the holiness of God, the conviction of sin intensifies and breeds in us an urgency for repentance (Isaiah 6:1-5; 2 Corinthians 7:10-11). Revival brings an intensity of God's grace which both demands and enables the abandonment of sin. We leave the well-worn trails of personal failure and sin and embark on the journey to Holiness! (Isaiah 35:8).

b. Humility and brokenness will be evident. In seasons of genuine revival, we experience a passion for purity, a clear conscience, and, above all, God's glory becomes so intense that no price is too great to pay.

c. Although not always enjoyable, embracing humility and experiencing brokenness is the only way to encounter God's holiness.

d. Just as Jesus endured the cross for the joy set before Him (Hebrews 12:2), so we must endure brokenness before God's joy can be restored to us (Psalm 51).

4. RELAUNCH | When we are walking in Extraordinary Wellness, we often go back and forth in the cycles, different seasons provide different pathways of support. However, the fruit of a healthy 4R 'cyclist' will ultimately produce a healthy living that is evident in our relationships, ministry, general satisfaction, and an authentic contentedness in your soul and mind. This is when we start to see things like:

a. Deliberate acts of reconciliation and restitution. No longer content to "let bygones be bygones," there will be a God-given zeal to obtain and maintain a clear conscience (Matthew 5:23-24; Acts 24:16).

b. No longer will we bring our gifts of worship and service to the altar while holding on to hurt, anger, or bitterness.

c. Evangelism will thrive. You will have a compulsion to be an influencer for Kingdom purposes, simply because of what He has and is doing within you! As God's Spirit rests on His church with renewed power, our witness to the world becomes palpable and credible.

d. Once bound by self-love, indifference, and fear of rejection, God's people now find new freedom, desire, and faith to share the gospel. Revival will propel us to Relaunch for the sake of completing the Great Commission.

Closing Prayer from Our Tribe to Yours

Father in Heaven,

Let Your name be great and famous among the nations! We ask that our Code Grape Culture readers walk in Your wellness, cultivate their Code Grape tribes, and call Code Grape! when they need support! We exist for Your Glory... so we choose to recognize and walk in Your blessings of guidance and understanding. We ask for wisdom in moments of need to seek Your Word for counsel, gather our sisters, and make healthy choices that would lead us into habits of Extraordinary Wellness! Help us choose to be bearers and bringers of Your Wellness into a World of great need.

God get glory from our lives!

Amen

Printed in Great Britain
by Amazon

35733566R00184